"If you've ever doubted the [...]
follows, *Embraced by the F[...]*
convince you. This book is a[...]

—T. SUZANNE ELLER, speaker and author of
The Woman I Am Becoming

"Through an in-depth look at the names of God, Susanne brings us to the dance floor to place our hand in the Father's hand and join Him in the dance of life. She shows us how to move to the rhyme of God's grace, sway to the melody of God's love, and follow in steps of God's leading. This book will make you feel loved and embraced by One who invites you to the greatest dance of all time."

—SHARON JAYNES, speaker and author of *The Power of a Woman's Words* and *Your Scars Are Beautiful to God*

"Susanne Scheppmann brings a fresh approach to the wonderful names of God. As you learn and grow through her insights, your heart will be moved by the reality of the Father who calls you into His embrace and calls you by your name."

—JENNIFER KENNEDY DEAN, speaker and author of best-selling *Live a Praying Life*

"In her newest book, *Embraced by the Father*, Susanne Scheppmann beautifully and powerfully weaves her must-read life story with God's heart of mercy, love, and redemption in a refreshing exploration of the names of God. Susanne has captured the very heart of God with her transparent and authentic application of His truth, personality, and characteristics in and through us in daily life. *Embraced by the Father* is a life-changing read that makes you fall in love with the Father all over again. Don't miss it!"

—MARY SOUTHERLAND, the Women's Ministry Motivator

"By exploring the attributes of God, Susanne offers a unique look into the grace and provision that can be ours. My desire to be embraced by God's grace was fulfilled through Susanne's shared wisdom, shared experiences, and poetic style that make her book the kind you want to share with your friends."

—MICCA CAMPBELL, speaker and author of *An Untroubled Heart*

"If you have ever longed for someone to notice you instantly, get to know you fully, and yet still love you unconditionally, you are not alone. Susanne Scheppmann's inspirational stories and intentional studies intricately woven into the fiber of *Embraced by the Father* will introduce you to the One who sees you, seeks you, and ultimately sustains you; your rescuer, redeemer, and reason for living. Experiencing *Embraced by the Father* will shift your life's perspective as you discover how a seemingly simple wallflower can be invited to the dance of a lifetime, then wistfully and wonderfully swept off of her feet by the King of the ball, never to be left lurking in the shadows again."

—KAREN EHMAN, national speaker for Proverbs 31 Ministries and Hearts at Home Conferences

"Susanne has seamlessly woven very personal and painful memories from her past with God's promises for each one of us. This life-changing book is for every woman who has ever struggled with painful memories, felt lonely, invisible, unworthy, or overlooked. Susanne will open your eyes and your heart to our God who sees you, heals you, provides for you, and embraces you. You will be forever changed."

—LEANN RICE, executive director of operations, Proverbs 31 Ministries

"Do you long to be seen, known, and loved by the Creator of the universe—your heavenly Father? With insight and compassion, Susanne Scheppmann introduces us to the God who reaches out His hand and draws us into an eternal, grace-filled dance with Himself. On every page, Susanne artfully weaves her own story with those of biblical men and women to demonstrate God's redemptive power in the lives of those the world sees as wallflowers, castoffs, and misfits. *Embraced by the Father* is filled with foundational truths about God every woman should know and hold dear to her heart."

—GLYNNIS WHITWER, author of *Work@home* and editor, *P31 Woman Magazine*, Proverbs 31 Ministries

"I glided along the dance floor of each chapter as Susanne metaphorically relates the names of God into dance steps. Her personal stories sprinkled throughout the book of hurt and triumph in trying to learn the moves as her heavenly Father guides her life are inspiring. Susanne's vulnerability is refreshing and makes me long to be embraced by my Father."

—LISA BOALT RICHARDSON, author of *Tea with a Twist* and *The World in Your Teacup*

SUSANNE SCHEPPMANN

Embraced
BY THE
Father

FINDING GRACE
IN THE NAMES OF GOD

NEW HOPE
PUBLISHERS

BIRMINGHAM, ALABAMA

New Hope® Publishers
P. O. Box 12065
Birmingham, AL 35202-2065
www.newhopepublishers.com
New Hope Publishers is a division of WMU®

Library of Congress Cataloging-in-Publication Data

Scheppmann, Susanne, 1954-
  Embraced by the Father : finding grace in the names of God / Susanne Scheppmann.
    p. cm.
  ISBN 978-1-59669-244-2 (hc)
  1. Christian women--Religious life. 2. God--Name--Biblical teaching. I. Title.
  BV4527.S273 2010
  242'.643--dc22

                              2009048457

Interior Design: Glynese Northam

ISBN-10: 1-59669-244-8
ISBN-13: 978-1-59669-244-2

N094139 • 0310 • 3M1

To Little Boy Blue
Michael Brandt — My Pumpkin

To the Chickadee Peeps
Emily Brandt — My Cupcake
Brianna Brandt — My Jelly Bean

Contents

Acknowledgments

Thank you to Andrea Mullins, Joyce Dinkins, Jonathan Howe, Ashley Stephens, Kathryne Solomon, Sherry Hunt, and Bruce Watford. You have made this project a joyful blessing to me. I pray that each of you experiences a special embrace from the Father as you continue your diligent work for His kingdom. Keep dancing!

Foreword

When I was eight years old, I remember wanting one thing more than anything else . . . my daddy's love. I remember standing beside his chair twirling around while my heart cried out for his attention. "Daddy, do you notice me? Daddy, am I beautiful? Daddy, am I your special little girl? Daddy, do you love me?" But my daddy never gave me those words of affirmation.

While my earthly daddy didn't notice me, my heavenly Daddy did.

It took years of heartbreak to discover this. Years of running from God in a fit of anger, hurt, feeling like a throwaway person. I wish I'd had Susanne's book during these years. Her gentle understanding of what it feels like to miss the embrace of the Father has given her divine wisdom to write the book you hold in your hands. This book is a treasure all women should read.

God promises to be a father to the fatherless and fill in the emotional gaps left behind from those who have abandoned us. Throughout my whole life, He has brought experiences my way that if I'll notice His hand in it, He'll reveal the depth of His love for me.

A couple of summers ago, I had the privilege to attend the Billy Graham Crusade in New York City with Billy's daughter, Ruth. Ruth and I have been friends and prayer partners for several years. We met and instantly bonded at a women's conference. To me, she is just Ruth, my friend who I laugh, cry, pray, and experience life with. I often forget about the celebrity status of her family.

But at the crusade there was no forgetting. Famous people were all around us as we made our way through the crowd to our reserved seats. My then 11-year-old daughter Hope, who was with me, kept exclaiming, "Mom, there are Amy Grant and Vince Gill! Mom, there are the Clintons who used to live in the White House!"

I kept wondering, *Who am I? I don't belong here with all these famous people.* But as the questions and doubt started to creep in, Ruth handed us badges to wear. All the famous people had them on. However, our badges had a gold star on the bottom. I quickly realized the meaning of this gold star as we walked past the famous people and sat with the Graham family. The gold star meant we were part of the family.

I sat down and wiped the tear that started to make its way down my cheek. I looked up to heaven and winked at my heavenly Daddy. His voice was so tender as He once again whispered to my heart, "Lysa, you are not the child of a broken parent who couldn't give you love. You are a child of God. Yes, Lysa, I notice you. Yes, Lysa, you are beautiful. Yes, Lysa, you are my special little girl. And yes, Lysa, I love you."

If you want to experience this kind of deep assurance, keep reading. You are about to experience what every girl big and little longs to be . . . embraced by the father.

—Lysa TerKeurst
President of Proverbs 31 Ministries, speaker,
author of *Becoming More Than a Good Bible Study Girl,* and
blogger at www.LysaTerKeurst.com.

Prelude

Cameras flashed like small lightning strikes. People smiled even as their eyes began to glisten with tears. A large circle formed around one solitary couple on the hardwood dance floor. The gray-haired gentleman reached tenderly toward the up-stretched arms extended from a wheelchair. He lifted the woman under her arms and braced her against his tuxedoed chest. She leaned into him and allowed his body to support her as they began to waltz slowly.

His face reflected a variety of emotions. He whispered in her ear, "Life has been good! *'A time to weep and a time to laugh, a time to mourn and a time to dance'* (Ecclesiastes 3:4). Sweetheart, tonight it's time to dance."

One, two, three. One, two, three. His feet, strong and sure, guided her steps. Her high-heeled shoes slid slowly across the parquet floor. Her head rested upon his shoulder and allowed him not only to take the lead, but also to sustain her withered body. She trusted him; he was her husband and lifetime dance partner.

Fifty years ago, she waltzed into his arms after she took his name in a joyous wedding ceremony. The vows had proven valid through better or worse, for richer or for poorer. Laughter had saturated their home. Rebellious children had brought times of weeping. A time of mourning relentlessly stalked them, but tonight was a time to dance. Now a final test presented itself in their lives. In sickness or in health, he would provide for her every need because she was still his bride. She possessed his name and with his name came security.

A thought struck me as I watched this scene transpire between my father-in-law and mother-in-law. We stir this same emotion in the heart of God. Many times throughout the Bible we are referred to as the bride of Christ. He sees us as His bride and reaches down to lift us up out of the quagmire of life. He offers us all the benefits of possessing His name. He says, *"I will rescue those who love me. I will protect those who trust in my name"* (Psalm 91:14 NLT).

God honors us by bestowing to us His name. He longs for us to lean into His heart — to trust Him. Every footstep we take in our faith brings us closer to knowing Him intimately. He reveals Himself throughout the Old Testament and New Testament by a variety of self-defining names. Each title presents the opportunity for us to respond to Him in faith. To reach up, take the strength of God's mighty arms, and allow Him to lead us in the different dance steps that life's rhythms provide.

Not only does the Lord desire for us to take His name, He longs for us to comprehend that He knows our name and loves us. He is personally involved in every detail of our lives. He loves us. He calls us by name.

> *The LORD who created you says: "Do not be afraid, for I have ransomed you. I have called you by name; you are mine. When you go through deep waters and great trouble, I will be with you. When you go through rivers of difficulty, you will not drown! When you walk through the fire of oppression, you will not be burned up; the flames will not consume you. For I am the LORD, your God, the Holy One of Israel,*

your Savior. . . . You are honored, and I love you"
(ISAIAH 43:1–4 NLT).

As women, we seek security. We want to feel loved and protected by someone who cares for us. For many women, myself included, our earthly fathers failed miserably in their role as daddies. God invites us, as our heavenly Father, to come dance with Him as a daughter might stand atop her daddy's feet to high step across the room. We may be widowed, divorced, or single by choice, but God desires for us to learn to dance through life on His everlasting arms as our eternal groom.

Do you find trusting God difficult? I did for many years. (And at times, doubts still arise.) Yet, my faith gained momentum as I began to know His character, His personality, and His power. He reveals all these traits through myriad names—the names of God.

So let's learn to know Him by name. Let's learn to take His name for our own security and peace of mind. Throughout the next few chapters, we will find Him as the God Who Sees when all seems dark. He will be the husband who provides when all else fails. His Banner of Love will cover us when we cower in fear from suffering. He will shepherd us when we lose our way.

God invites us to dance in His eternal promises and security.

So, do you want to take some dance lessons? Do you want to inherit the benefits provided by the names of the Most High God? Will you accept the outstretched arms of the One who loves you? Yes? Well then, let's dance. One, two, three, one, two . . .

THE *Wallflower Waltz*

*H*e began to walk toward me. His smile sparkled with the yet unasked question. The drumbeat of my heart rang in my ears as it pounded out the music. My adolescent heart fluttered with anxious excitement. My face flushed in anticipation. I wiped my sweaty hands on my skirt, knowing that soon this handsome quarterback would be taking my hand to lead me onto the dance floor.

His grin deepened as he strolled by me to the perky blond cheerleader who giggled behind me.

"Wanna dance?" he asked.

Their hands linked as he led her to the dance floor. I felt myself disappear into the background. My heart sank as I understood that he never saw me standing on the glossy yellow-wood floor of the high school gym. I was invisible.

Can you relate? Maybe it wasn't at a dance, but being the last girl picked from your fourth-grade class to play soccer. Or perhaps you are instinctively quiet and shy; you feel invisible in the world of social butterflies. Maybe your husband plops on the tan leather couch clutching the remote control and ignores you every evening.

As women, we all feel unseen during times our lives. Whether we're a world-traveling superstar or a woman who

17

feels trapped inside her home by toddlers, rest assured we are not unseen by God. It's hard to comprehend that the God of the universe is aware of our every movement, but He is. God sees us when we believe we are invisible. He observes our every move even when we attempt to be undetectable.

A FLECK OF PINK FLANNEL

I grew up in northern Utah. My hometown was small and behind the times. (Even today, it appears to be caught in a time warp of the 1950s.) When I was growing up, the town was populated predominantly by Latter-Day Saints, more commonly known as Mormons. Mormons hold strong moral ethics. They stress exceptional family values in order to be able to be in a good relationship with God.

Oh, boy! That left me believing I would never be close to God. My father savored alcohol, cigarettes, and my mother's best friend, who lived next door. A fourth-generation alcoholic, he had no clue how to be a faithful husband or a good father. He would disappear for days, only to come home in a drunken stupor. Family dysfunction and spiritual darkness hovered in our home.

My mentally ill mother spoke in garbled phrases of schizophrenic fear. She loved me desperately and tried her best to care for me. However, life centered around the committee of voices she heard in her head. On "good" days, she would venture out to fortune-tellers with me in tow. We would traipse into a dimly lit, incensed-filled room where a gypsy-looking woman would lay strange cards down before us. She would gaze solemnly at my mom and then whisper what the cards foretold for my future. I remember feeling frightened, but also drawn into the mystic atmosphere. Tarot cards and horoscopes guided our day-to-day activities.

Besides the darkness of the occult that infiltrated our home, so did human dysfunction. I remember waking up one night around three in the morning. I heard my drunken dad screaming filthy obscenities and the sound of glass breaking. Suddenly, my bedroom door flew open and my wild-eyed mother yanked me out of bed. She half-carried and half-dragged me through the hallway. She shoved me out the front door and together we ran down the middle of the street screaming for help. Our morally religious neighbors must have looked at our home as a freak show.

The confused and scared little girl in me believed that God didn't see what happened in my home. He didn't know about the little girl in pink flowered flannel pajamas who sobbed with frightened bewilderment. *Why wasn't my life like my girlfriends'? Their parents didn't fight. They slept through the night without fisticuffs happening in the kitchen.* I reasoned it must be because they were good and I was bad. God loved and cared for them. He watched over my friends, but not me. I appeared only as a speck of pink flannel on the cool moonlit pavement. I was invisible to God.

However, my impression of God's eyesight was mistaken. He doesn't need contacts, glasses, or eye surgery to see invisible little wallflowers in the dredges of life. God sees every little girl, in every circumstance, everywhere.

A Speck of Sand

Thousands of years ago, a young girl, Hagar, lived in the deserts of the Middle East. The Bible grants us a bit of information concerning Hagar:

Now Sarai, Abram's wife, had borne him no children. But she had an Egyptian maidservant named Hagar; so she said to Abram, "The LORD has kept me from having children. Go, sleep with my maidservant; perhaps I can build a family through her."

Abram agreed to what Sarai said. So after Abram had been living in Canaan ten years, Sarai his wife took her Egyptian maidservant Hagar and gave her to her husband to be his wife. He slept with Hagar, and she conceived.

When she knew she was pregnant, she began to despise her mistress. Then Sarai said to Abram, "You are responsible for the wrong I am suffering. I put my servant in your arms, and now that she knows she is pregnant, she despises me. May the LORD judge between you and me."

"Your servant is in your hands," Abram said. "Do with her whatever you think best." Then Sarai mistreated Hagar; so she fled from her.

The angel of the LORD found Hagar near a spring in the desert; it was the spring that is beside the road to Shur. And he said, "Hagar, servant of Sarai, where have you come from, and where are you going?"

"I'm running away from my mistress Sarai," she answered.

Then the angel of the LORD told her, "Go back to your mistress and submit to her." The angel added, "I will so increase your descendants that they will be too numerous to count." . . . She gave this name to the LORD who spoke to her: "You are the God

*who sees me," for she said, "I have now seen the One
who sees me"* (GENESIS 16:1–13).

*She gave this name to the
LORD who spoke to her:
"You are the God who
sees me," for she said,
"I have now seen the
One who sees me"
(Genesis 16:13).*

We read that Hagar was a slave owned by a mistress named Sarai. Sarai and her husband, Abram, traveled extensively during their marriage. So, let's use our imaginations to pretend that Hagar needs a passport to travel with them. The passport application might appear as follows:

Name: Hagar

Sex: Female

Occupation: Slave

Nationality: Egyptian

Age: Healthy childbearing age

Next of Kin: Sarai — Slave owner

Very little is known about her childhood, but we can speculate on some of it. First, let's surmise how the young Egyptian girl became a slave. Slavery was an accepted practice in the ancient Middle East. Perhaps, marauders who, in turn, sold her as a servant to the wealthy Abram and Sarai, captured Hagar.

On the other hand, Hagar's parents may have even been the ones to sell her into a lifetime of servitude for a few bucks. Female children held very little value in ancient societies. To sell a child into bondage as a slave meant a few more loaves of bread on the table for a while.

We cannot know for certain, but we can imagine the thoughts of a young girl trapped in a life of servitude. Surely, questions surfaced in Hagar's mind: *Does anyone truly care for me? Where are the gods of Egypt? Do the gods not see my suffering?*

Then her crabby, barren mistress comes up with the idea of having a child through the uterus of Hagar—a surrogate mother. Because *in vitro* fertilization had not been developed yet, Hagar was sent to the tent of Abram, so she could bear a child for Sarai. She was probably not much older than a young adolescent. Picture the scene of the innocent girl going to sleep with a man who is at least 85. Basically, we can deduce that Abram had sex with her, but held no tenderness, compassion, or love for the girl young enough to be his great-granddaughter. Again, Hagar must have felt invisible. Only a servant girl to Sarai, only a fresh young lass to a crusty old man, and only a body to produce a child she could not call her own.

NOW I AM SOMEBODY

Hagar's youthful and fertile body accepts the job of surrogate mother. The pregnancy produces a feeling of importance. "Oh, now I am somebody!" she says. "I hold in my womb the longed-for son of Mr. Abram. He will see me now! Surely, he will love and care for me now." Hormonal pride floods her. She no longer perceives herself as a grain of sand in a vast desert; now she holds the key to prestige and honor within her lithe body.

Hagar was pregnant with the heir of rich, old Abram. Hagar began to despise and taunt Sarai, because she felt safe within her good fortune. The spotlight of social prominence shown brilliantly on her enlarged belly. *Yes, the fertility gods of Egypt have shown their favor on me,* she must have thought.

However, envy and women do not make a compatible pair. Hagar didn't even have time to enjoy her moment in the desert sun. Her insolence infuriated her mistress. Sarai rushed to her husband to complain bitterly. She actually accused Abram of creating the problem. (We're talking female catfight!) Abram only desired peace in his tent. So he shrugged his shoulders and said, "Since she is your servant, you may deal with her as you see fit" (Genesis 16:6 NLT). Sarai saw fit to abuse Hagar. She retaliated against the pride and pregnancy of young Hagar. Hagar fled.

EL ROI — THE GOD WHO SEES A SPECK

Pregnant Hagar fled into the desert. Perhaps she studied the sun and stars, seeking astrological guidance for her desperate situation. Instead of "the gods" directing her, Hagar's predicament was seen and understood by the one and only God.

The Lord God knew everything about Hagar. He knew her name, her owner's name, and Hagar's job description. Yet He questioned her, "Hagar, servant of Sarai, where have you come from, and where are you going?" God queried Hagar, so she could understand herself and her circumstances. I wonder what went through Hagar's mind as she replied, "I am running away from my mistress Sarai." The Lord God obviously was already familiar with her mistress and why she was running away. He was the God who saw her in her miserable life.

Suddenly she realized she was not invisible, but important in the eyes of the Lord. I am sure her heart overflowed with peace and comfort as she declared, "You are the God who sees me," for she said, "I have now seen the One who sees me."

INVITATION TO WALTZ

I resonate with Hagar's story. Although when I was a child I felt as if God didn't see me, I was wrong. God saw my tender heart. He was working in my life in subtle ways.

My parents never attended church. They celebrated Christmas and Easter, but it was only with the worldview of Santa Claus and the Easter Bunny. Nevertheless, God opened up doors for me to begin to be acquainted with Him. My young girlfriends invited me to go to church with them. So, I went to the Methodist church because they served doughnuts on white paper napkins after Sunday School. I attended the Catholic Church for pancake breakfasts. In my childish estimation, the pancakes ranked higher than the doughnuts on the menu. The Baptist church held Vacation Bible School each summer and it was fun. Slowly, I began to feel the Spirit of God woo me toward Himself. Even though I could not have verbalized it, I sensed the importance of the Word of God in my life. I recall asking for a Bible on my tenth birthday. My parents glanced at one another with the look, *What an odd child we have!*

THE ONE WHO SAW ME

Eventually, my parents divorced and my mother proceeded deeper into occult practices. My mother died at age 36 from secondary causes attributed to her mental illness. At that time, I was 14. I knew only a little about God, but I despised Him for allowing my mother to die. Hatred and bitterness filled my heart, and I fled into a desert of adolescent rebellion.

However, God saw the gangly, stringy-haired, wayward teen. No matter how I tried to run from God, it was impossible to flee from His presence. Psalm 139 states this truth with poetic accuracy:

> *Where can I go from your Spirit?*
> > *Where can I flee from your presence?*
> *If I go up to the heavens, you are there;*
> > *if I make my bed in the depths, you are there.*
> *If I rise on the wings of the dawn,*
> > *if I settle on the far side of the sea,*
> *even there your hand will guide me,*
> > *your right hand will hold me fast* (7–10).

If I settle on the far side of the sea, even there your hand will guide me, your right hand will hold me fast (Psalm 139:9–10).

Although I tried to be an invisible wallflower in the eyes of God, He never let me out of His sight. He knew that I was angry, hurt, and full of despair. In His mercy, His hand kept guiding me even though I was on the run in a desert of rebellion.

Yes, no matter how much we may feel invisible or try to flee from El Roi, He is right there waiting for us to understand that He wants to waltz with us wallflowers. He offers His hand to guide us through the uncertainties of life, step by complex step. And then when the music begins to fade, He will lead His children into the certainty of eternal life in heaven.

This precept is illustrated several times in the New Testament. One of my favorite examples is of the skeptic Nathanael.

Philip went off to look for Nathanael and told him, "We have found the very person Moses and the prophets wrote about! His name is Jesus, the son of Joseph from Nazareth."

"Nazareth!" exclaimed Nathanael. "Can anything good come from there?"

"Just come and see for yourself," Philip said.

As they approached, Jesus said, "Here comes an honest man — a true son of Israel."

"How do you know about me?" Nathanael asked.

And Jesus replied, "I could see you under the fig tree before Philip found you."

Nathanael replied, "Teacher, you are the Son of God — the King of Israel!"

Jesus asked him, "Do you believe all this just because I told you I had seen you under the fig tree? You will see greater things than this."

(JOHN 1:45–50 NLT)

Jesus sees us before we ever begin to see Him. Many times someone unexpected leads us onto the dance floor to become the partner of Jesus, just as Philip went to Nathanael with the invitation to come and see Jesus the Christ. That is how my invitation to dance came too.

Strange as it seems, my alcoholic father married a Christian woman named Kay. She loved me as my own mother had. Her love remained steady, no matter how horribly I treated her. She told me about Jesus and His dying on the Cross for me. Her words did not influence me, but her actions did. I observed how she used the Bible as a handbook for life. I witnessed her faith in action. I felt the Spirit of God's love flow out of her toward me.

I ridiculed her, as Hagar did Sarai. But unlike Sarai, Kay loved me anyway. Kay recognized the confusion and hurt of a wallflower girl. She saw me with the eyes of God, El Roi, the God who sees. She loved me into the arms of Jesus.

One night in our dark, dank basement, I accepted Christ's offer to become His child. I asked Jesus to come into my heart as my Lord and God. Instantly, I began an eternal dance with Jesus the Christ — the God who sees. No longer an invisible wallflower, I allowed Him to lead me into an eternal heavenly waltz.

However, the story of God originates before El Roi; it starts with creation — a world designed for dancing. In the beginning . . .

Dance Lesson

When have you felt like a wallflower?

Read Psalm 139:1–16.

How do these verses dispel the notion of your being a wallflower?

Has there been a time when you have tried to flee from God?

Hindsight is 20/20 vision. Looking back, can you see how El Roi has asked you to dance with Him?

Perhaps He is inviting you now. How will you say yes to Jesus Christ?

Here's how to RSVP to the invitation of the Wallflower Waltz:

Lord Jesus, I know You are the God who sees me. I want You to be my dance instructor for life, both now and eternally. I know I have made many missteps in life. Please come and be my Lord and Savior for all eternity. Right now, I want to trust in You in order to receive Your eternal life. I will follow Your lead and teaching. I want to become a follower of Christ. You will be my instructor and guide for all eternity. I ask this in Your name, the God who sees, amen.

Advanced Dance Lesson

Read Luke 19:1–9.

Describe how Jesus demonstrates that He is El Roi, the God who sees, to Zacchaeus.

How did Zacchaeus respond to Jesus in the following verses?

Verses 3–4:

Verse 6:

Verse 8:

How did Jesus respond to Zacchaeus's proclamation?

Verses 9–10:

Using Psalm 139 for inspiration, write a closing prayer to El Roi, the God who sees.

The Wallflower Waltz Journal Page

Jot down your thoughts about El Roi — the God who sees you.

~~~~~~

~~~~~~

~~~~~~

~~~~~~

~~~~~~

~~~~~~

~~~~~~

~~~~~~

~~~~~~

~~~~~~

~~~~~~

~~~~~~

~~~~~~

~~~~~~

~~~~~~

~~~~~~

~~~~~~

~~~~~~

Hebrew name: El Roi

Definition: You are the God who sees me.

Modern name: God who sees me

The Waltz

Ballroom dancing as we now know started with the introduction of the waltz. The word *waltz* comes from the old German and it means to turn and to glide. The waltz began as early as the seventeenth century, but was made popular by Johann Strauss. His "Blue Danube" is probably the most well-known waltz music around the world.

The waltz is a smooth dance, traveling around the line of dance. It is characterized primarily by its rise and fall action written in ¾ meter. The shoulders move smoothly, parallel with the floor, not up and down. The head should turn in the direction of the turn; otherwise the man's head is upright and looking over the right shoulder of the woman.

Ballroom OF Stars

The maggots squirmed as the light flooded the room. The health inspector stepped over the heaps of trash that appeared the moment he opened the front door. His Adam's apple bobbed up and down as he tried to reswallow the bile that slid up his throat caused by the rancid stench. He gulped hard and proceeded stoically farther into my home.

Four cats scooted underneath the couch. Three dogs ran to greet the health inspector, his assistants, my father, and myself. The old poodle, Toodles, nipped angrily at five pairs of ankles. The Chihuahua barked ferociously, but stayed at a distance. My favorite dog, Todd, leapt up, eager for anyone's attention. I patted his black head and tagged along behind my embarrassed father who followed the three health department officials. With each step farther into the disgust, I saw their eyes widen, their nostrils quiver, and disbelief wash across their faces.

As the procession moved to the kitchen, their senses began to numb. The sink, stove, and counters were buried under what seemed a landfill of debris. Half-filled bottles of unidentified liquid sat on the kitchen table next to plates of half-eaten cat food. To me it didn't stink — it was just the smell of home. I had become accustomed to it, although I did like to burn patchouli candles in my own room to help sweeten the air.

The first door on the right was my bedroom. At 13, I was proud of my room. It had bright-colored paisley curtains, teal shag carpeting, and black light posters hanging on the wall. (It was the 1970s!) The floor was fairly free of debris. Todd, my dog, scooted past us and jumped on the unmade bed. Although my bedroom wasn't clean, it wasn't any worse than most teenage girls' rooms. I saw the inspector shrug his shoulders as if to say, "Well, at least that room *seems* normal."

We started back down the hallway. On the left side, a door stood ajar. A thicker intensity of stench oozed from the room—the bathroom. The inspector pushed the door open until all eyes could see the source of the corpselike smell. Piles of clothes carpeted the floor with just a small linoleum pathway alongside the tub to the toilet. The laundry that overflowed from the tops of the washer and dryer had become the indoor kitty litter box. Cat urine and feces plastered the now ruined clothes.

I heard the head inspector gasp, then gag. Then he said, "This home is condemned!" He shook his foot and I watched a maggot slither back into its familiar home of animal filth.

I had become used to the trash, the stench, the pets, and even the maggots—it was my home. It hadn't always been like this, of course. It happened slowly over an extended time. After my parents' divorce, my mother's mental illness progressed at a rapid pace. I was in middle school. The desire to be popular overtook me as I attended the after-school dances and participated in teenage relationships—cliquey girlfriends and obtuse, cute guys. I didn't pay attention to the slow destruction happening at home. I just wanted to dance on the polished gym floor and allow the pounding music to push me into a hunky boy's arms.

Instead, each time I was rejected by a group of fickle girls or ignored by the latest school heartthrob, I brought home a pet.

My mother didn't mind. They kept her company, as she became a mental shut-in.

The county official hastily picked up the phone hanging on the Harvest Gold wall and dialed animal control. The man looked at me coldly as if I had purposely created all the filth and contamination. He said, "Call the dogs to you." He glanced over my head to my father, "We'll catch the cats."

My heart broke as I realized what was happening. My world came crashing down as the harshness of the uncaring adults rushed into my broken heart. These men were taking my pets — the one last comfort in my adolescent turmoil.

Illusions

At 13, I ignored the horror of reality and pursued the illusion. (I still do sometimes.) But I think everyone has or does the same thing. In adolescence, I searched for my illusions on a polished wood floor in a room that reeked with boys' sweat and girls' persnickety attitudes. I sought a prince-boy while gyrating to Jimi Hendrix's "Purple Haze." It was a futile attempt. My futility then sought comfort in the warm silky fur of my pets.

As my friends and I matured, the mirage of happiness pirouetted just out of emotional reach. Some of my friends turned to smoked-filled bars with pole-dancing. Others were put behind bars because of drugs.

In the Beginning

God never intended our world to be a dirty, darkened place where we slink about in a sin-saddened humanity. His original dance floor was fragrant with lush beauty and light that sparkled with His glory and reflected His perennial purpose for us.

At the dawn of time, God created the perfect home of beauty. He desired this world and our lives to be filled with lush beauty. The first time we read the word *God* in the Bible is in the very first verse. Genesis 1:1 reads, "In the beginning God created the heavens and the earth." The word *God* in the original Hebrew is *Elohim.* The complete definition of Elohim, or God, conveys the image of the one true God, a regal creator who creates perfection out of nothing and rules compassionately with majesty and absolute power. And so with all this Elohim ability, He created a beautiful ballroom for His children to enjoy — the earth — our world.

"In the beginning God created the heavens and the earth" (Genesis 1:1).

Here's an abbreviated summary of God's creation found in Genesis 1 from *The Message*:

- *God created the Heavens and the Earth — all you see.*
- *God spoke: "Light!" And light appeared. God saw that light was good and separated light from dark.*
- *God spoke: "Separate! Water-beneath-Heaven, gather into one place; Land appear!" And there it was. God saw that it was good.*
- *God spoke: "Earth, green up!" Earth produced green seed-bearing plants, all varieties.... And there it was.... God saw that it was good.*

- *God spoke: "Lights! Come out! Shine in Heaven's sky!" Oversee Day and Night to separate light and dark." God saw that it was good.*
- *God spoke: "Swarm, Ocean, with fish and all sea life.... Earth, generate life!" And there it was: wild animals of every kind, cattle of all kinds, and every sort of reptile and bug. God saw that it was good.*
- *God spoke: "Let us make human beings in our image, make them reflecting our nature...." Reflecting God's nature He created them male and female. God blessed them.*
- *And there it was. God looked over everything he had made, it was so good, so very good!*

So there was Earth—a perfect paradise—a divine dance floor. Our world, our home, and "it was so good, so very good!" It was a place created for male and female to dance throughout in blissful joy. But then, the female, Eve, decided she needed just a bit more. Her illusion was to be like God. She wrongly desired knowledge beyond what God desired for her.

And we know the end of her story. She just couldn't resist the temptation to snack at the one forbidden tree. She allowed herself to be deceived; she grabbed the fruit and bit. Adam, her prince-boy, nibbled at the delicacy too. And so began the slide into the dark side of life, away from the outstretched arm and heart of God. Her misstep caused every person afterward to search out and explore the illusion of happiness that sin offers.

THE RENAISSANCE

My railroad-working, hard-drinking father swore at the health inspector. My dad argued he could bring the condemned home back to livability. He insisted they give him 60 days, then come and reinspect. They agreed reluctantly to the proposal.

My dad began with a shovel and a large trash can. Load by load he shoveled the trash, the clothes, the feces, and maggots out of the house. He ripped out the carpet and padding. He tore off the baseboards. The wallpaper was scraped off inch by inch. Every Harvest Gold appliance was carted off to the dump. Bleach saturated every permissible inch of the structure.

Then, fresh paint covered the walls. New teal shag carpet (complete with a plastic carpet rake) was laid. Kitchen carpet replaced the stained linoleum. Avocado green appliances sparkled with a sanitary gleam. (Remember, this was the 1970s at their finest.) Not a pet in sight, no maggots to be found — the home passed the state health criteria. My father and I were allowed to move back into the house.

However, the sadness and depression remained in every room. The house had been renovated, but it was the same old home. I longed for my mother. I missed my pets. I felt alienated from my dad. I continued to seek refuge and happiness with my immature friendships, but no critters were allowed through the door.

The surroundings appeared homey, but my father and I didn't know how to clean up the emotional debacle that remained. No disinfectant could sanitize the loneliness out of the house. Fresh paint wouldn't cover up the emotional scars. New carpet couldn't soften the thud of disdain that I felt for my father. He didn't know how, nor did he even want to fix the father-daughter relationship.

The renaissance of relationship would take decades. My 14-year-old fantasy for "normal" remained unfulfilled, but thankfully, my living conditions had improved. Life on earth will never be perfect. There will always be sin, sickness, and sorrow, but God can clean up the debris and create an atmosphere of emotional and spiritual health.

A REGAL RENAISSANCE

Thankfully for us, God knows how to bring about a total renaissance. His renovation restores everything physically, emotionally, and spiritually. He is preparing a new home for us — a perfect place of celebration. He will fix what humanity has broken into miserable pieces. God is going to provide us with a completely new dance floor. Incredible? Here's the description of the renaissance of God's perfect creation.

> *I saw Heaven and earth new-created. Gone the first Heaven, gone the first earth, gone the sea. . . .*
>
> *I heard a voice thunder from the Throne: "Look! Look! God has moved into the neighborhood, making his home with men and women! They're his people, he's their God. He'll wipe every tear from their eyes. Death is gone for good — tears gone, crying gone, pain gone — all the first order of things gone"* (REVELATION 21:1–4 THE MESSAGE).

In his popular book *Heaven,* Randy Alcorn writes, "Will we cry in heaven? The Bible says, 'He will wipe away every tear from their eyes; and there will no longer be *any* death; there will no longer be any mourning, or crying, or pain' (Revelation 21:4, NASB, emphasis added). These are the tears of suffering over sin and death, the tears of oppressed people, the cries of the poor, the widow, the orphaned, the unborn, and the persecuted. God will wipe away the tears of racial injustice. Such crying shall be no more."

The pain and sorrow of this rickety old ballroom of earth will disappear, but imagine the dance floor of heaven. There will be no more tears, pain, or death. Alcorn continues with his thoughts of what the eternal dance floor might be like. "I imagine our first glimpse of Heaven will cause us to similarly gasp in amazement and delight. That first gasp will likely be followed by many more as we continually encounter new sights in that endlessly wonderful place."

I'm excited. After decades of waiting, I will step onto the newly finished dance floor of heaven and hear God say to me,

> *"Again you will take up your tambourines*
> *and go out to dance with the joyful.*
> *Then maidens will dance and be glad,*
> *young men and old as well.*
> *I will turn their mourning into gladness"*
> (JEREMIAH 31:4, 13).

God will say these words to you too. No matter how wretched your home, your family, or your life, God will bring about a regal renaissance to you in heaven if you'll let Him. All the filth will be washed away. You will be purified not by household bleach, but by the purity of God Himself.

BROKEN LIVES REBUILT

But what about now?

From a personal look at my life all those years ago, it all looked like shards of shattered glass. My mother's mental illness followed by her death, my alcoholic father, our house that was not a home, all hardly prepared me for a life of happiness or success. Statistically, as an adult my life should have been a mess. (And on my own, it would have been.) But because I began a personal relationship with God at the age of 15, He recreated me.

He turned my sufferings into beauty and blessings. I didn't march down the same old family history channel of behavior repetition. Instead, He taught me to dance in an arena of new life.

Another example of a divine renaissance is Joni Eareckson Tada. Joni, a quadriplegic for more than 40 years, paints and writes from a wheelchair. Her life is an example of extreme destruction, but divine renovation. She writes in *Heaven: Your Real Home*, "Suffering is no failure of God's plan. True, it is part of the curse, along with death, disease, and destruction. But before God comes back to close the curtain on suffering, it is meant to be redeemed."

How has God redeemed the heartache in Joni's life? Marriage to a wonderfully supportive husband, Ken, came after her devastating paralysis. She has authored countless books and painted a myriad of watercolor artwork that are in popular demand. (She uses a tool in her mouth to paint and type.) She is the founder of Joni and Friends (JAF) Ministries — an outreach to the disabled around the world. Joni is an apt example of what our God — the Creator God — can create out of what appears to be, from a human point of view, complete devastation.

God is in the business of human redemption and restoration. Joni's life, my life, and yours can illustrate the truth of Isaiah 61:3–4.

The oil of gladness
   instead of mourning,
and a garment of praise
   instead of a spirit of despair.
They will be called oaks of righteousness,
   a planting of the LORD
   for the display of his splendor.

They will rebuild the ancient ruins
   and restore the places long devastated;
they will renew the ruined cities
   that have been devastated for generations.

God has the ability to build new lives from any type of suffering — whether for a day or for generations. I know, because He restored my dysfunction to normalcy — well, at least as normal as I can be here on earth. It didn't happen overnight. I stumbled, I fell, but He lifted me and set me on my feet again.

> *They will rebuild the ancient ruins and restore the places long devastated; they will renew the ruined cities that have been devastated for generations (Isaiah 61:4).*

God created for me a new life from a home that was broken in many ways. He removed the maggots of dysfunction from my life and replaced them with His Spirit. He cleaned me up and placed me on a ballroom floor of a recreated life.

And He set my feet to dancing — even when they were two left feet struggling to learn the steps of restoration.

Dance Lesson

Read Genesis 1 and John 1:1–18.

Compare the two passages. How are they similar? How are they different?

Reread John 14:14 and John 14:27.

Who do we discover is the Word?

What in your life needs to be rebuilt or re-created?

Can you trust Jesus, the Word, to help you dance in a new ballroom of stars? Why or why not?

45

Advanced Dance Lesson

Read John 14:1–3.

Write John 14:1 in your own words.

How does this comfort you?

What did Jesus say He was going away to do?

Read Revelation 21:10–27.

What are your thoughts of this description of heaven?

Ballroom of Stars Journal Page

Jot down your thoughts about God — the Creator God.

~~~~~~~~~~~~~~~~~~~~~~~~~~~~~~~~
~~~~~~~~~~~~~~~~~~~~~~~~~~~~~~~~
~~~~~~~~~~~~~~~~~~~~~~~~~~~~~~~~
~~~~~~~~~~~~~~~~~~~~~~~~~~~~~~~~
~~~~~~~~~~~~~~~~~~~~~~~~~~~~~~~~
~~~~~~~~~~~~~~~~~~~~~~~~~~~~~~~~
~~~~~~~~~~~~~~~~~~~~~~~~~~~~~~~~
~~~~~~~~~~~~~~~~~~~~~~~~~~~~~~~~
~~~~~~~~~~~~~~~~~~~~~~~~~~~~~~~~
~~~~~~~~~~~~~~~~~~~~~~~~~~~~~~~~
~~~~~~~~~~~~~~~~~~~~~~~~~~~~~~~~
~~~~~~~~~~~~~~~~~~~~~~~~~~~~~~~~
~~~~~~~~~~~~~~~~~~~~~~~~~~~~~~~~
~~~~~~~~~~~~~~~~~~~~~~~~~~~~~~~~
~~~~~~~~~~~~~~~~~~~~~~~~~~~~~~~~
~~~~~~~~~~~~~~~~~~~~~~~~~~~~~~~~
~~~~~~~~~~~~~~~~~~~~~~~~~~~~~~~~
~~~~~~~~~~~~~~~~~~~~~~~~~~~~~~~~
~~~~~~~~~~~~~~~~~~~~~~~~~~~~~~~~
~~~~~~~~~~~~~~~~~~~~~~~~~~~~~~~~
~~~~~~~~~~~~~~~~~~~~~~~~~~~~~~~~

Hebrew name: ELOHIM

Definition: SUPREME, ETERNAL, AND CREATOR

Modern name: GOD

Dance Room Decor

When decorating for a dance or party, consider what will prompt the guests to remember the occasion and say, "It was good!" Use various techniques that will enhance the five senses — touch, taste, sight, hearing, and smell.

Two Left Feet

The accordion wheezed in and out with the melody, while the tuba burped out the rhythm — *oompah-pah oompah-pah*. The oompah band, dressed in traditional Bavarian style attire — red knickers, canary-yellow knee socks, small hunter-green vests, and green felt caps with bright red feathers wagging from the brim — played for the crowd. Each musician clutched his instrument as if it were his lover and then nodded toward the audience, encouraging them toward the dance floor.

Several members of my extended family stared at the video recording of my father-in-law's retirement party. We sat mesmerized as we relived the gaiety of those priceless moments. With oompahs playing in the background, we watched ourselves hitch arms and jig in a large circle. And, of course, human nature as it is, we all wanted to see ourselves dance to oompah music.

Suddenly, I spied myself. I thought, *Ugh!* Unfortunately, my father-in-law paused the video and said with an air of surprise, "I didn't know you had two left feet."

And there you have it — my secret came out. My husband's family is musical. They sing and play musical instruments — drums, trumpets, the organ, etc. And they all dance like Fred Astaire and Ginger Rogers. My husband knew, but otherwise I had kept my two left feet a secret. But now it was on video and there was no denying it. I possess no sense of rhythm. I can't carry a tune. My feet do not dance.

AUTOHARPS, GUITARS, AND BEBOP

This ineptness began to display itself when I was a child.

"Pick me!" my hand said as it waved high above my head.

My fourth-grade teacher locked eyes with me and smiled. She asked, "Susanne, would you like to play the Autoharp for our Christmas play?"

"Yes!" I said. I would have rather played the Autoharp than strutted as the leading lady across the stage.

Thrilled to be chosen, I chose to stay in at recess to learn. I grabbed the stringed instrument and placed the melodious treasure across my lap. Its polished wood gleamed. I pressed the black and white buttons and strummed the strings. It sounded beautiful. I practiced every moment I could find after that first afternoon of musical rapture.

Two weeks later, my teacher stood beside me. She listened thoughtfully and then said, "Susanne, I think that I need you in a different area of our production. I must have someone I can depend on to switch the lights on and off on cue. You're the person I trust. I guess Mary Lou will have to play the Autoharp."

Within myself, I knew it was because she didn't think my musical ability was up to par for our Christmas event. I submissively learned to click the proper light switches behind the black velvet curtains of the stage.

However, I wouldn't allow myself to be discouraged. The next year I begged for guitar lessons. So, my parents bought me a cheap, used guitar and I trotted off to music lessons. After only six weeks, I overheard the guitar instructor whisper to my dad, "You're wasting your money. She can't *'hear'* the music." My lessons ended.

Then I entered my early teen years and my next endeavor was modern dance lessons. The bebopper inside my head flourished on the dance floor. However, my physically toned, tanned, and tenacious dance teacher also gave up on me. Exasperated, she told me she was incapable of teaching me what I needed to know about dance, especially rhythm.

Now as an adult, I realize this—I have *amusia*. (It doesn't mean being amused by something.) *Amusia* is the inability of a person's brain to process and store the information of musical notes, pitch, tones, tunes, and rhythms. Music is like a foreign language—it's great to listen to, but people with amusia can't "speak" it. They cannot carry a tune when they sing or keep to the beat when they dance. That's me! I can't carry a tune in a bucket. I am deficient in music recognition and the ability to reproduce the right notes and beats.

Amusia is not an amusing malady. Here is the weird thing—I don't just like music; I adore it. My iPod holds hundreds of worship and praise songs. The earbuds protrude from my head like two large plastic pimples. Music is for my soul as air is to my lungs.

Up until middle age, I tried and tried to learn to understand the world of music, but now I just enjoy listening to it. I recognize my musical disability and believe that when I reach heaven, I will sing with the best of the best—but not now.

OUR DEFICIENCY, HIS SUFFICIENCY

Everyone has some type of deficiency. God created us that way. Why? So that we must depend on Him as the God Almighty in our lives. In the Hebrew language He is *El Shaddai*—*the All Sufficient One.*

The first time we find the name of God as El Shaddai, the All Sufficient One, is with Abraham and Sarah. God promises to be sufficient and to prove that all things are possible, even when the situation appears hopeless. Here's a little background information on Abraham and Sarah.

This story follows on the heels of pregnant Hagar, the wallflower, whom God Almighty saw in her unfortunate and unfair circumstances. Again, we see Abram, now called Abraham. God changed Abram's name to reflect the change that was going to occur in his life. "No longer will you be called Abram; your name will be Abraham, for I have made you a father of many nations" (Genesis 17:5). God also changed Abraham's wife's name from Sarai to Sarah.

Now Abraham was 99 years old, his wife, Sarah, was 90, and they were childless. I imagine that both Abraham and Sarah were shrunken. The way old people seem to shrink into their wrinkles—wrinkles that loom larger year after year until they consume the original face—and their height diminishes from tall and erect to hunched diminutiveness like a rotting apple left hanging on the tree. Abraham was old, but Sarah was old and deficient.

Sarah's deficiency? She had not provided Abraham a child—specifically, a son. In ancient times, barrenness was a family's greatest misfortune. It didn't matter how their gold might glitter. It made no difference if they wore fine clothing woven with threads of purple denoting elevated social status. A son was the treasure sought after, longed for, and prayed for as a drowning person gasps for air. This was the case for Abraham and Sarah. Blessings were of no use if there was not a son to whom to pass down the inheritance. Genesis 15:2 (NLT) reveals the despair of Abraham, "O Sovereign LORD, what good are all your blessings when I don't even have a son? Since I don't have a son, Eliezer of Damascus, a servant in my household, will inherit all my wealth."

Can you hear the resignation in Abraham's words? He had given up on his and Sarah's ability to produce an heir for his God-given blessings. But the Lord was about to prove the power of His newly revealed name — God Almighty or, in the Hebrew, El Shaddai. But what does God Almighty mean to Abraham, Sarah, and us? In *Titles of a Triune God*, author Herbert Stevenson explains it this way: "God Almighty . . . is . . . a most inadequate translation which quite misses the profound implications of the wondrous title, and the revelation of the love of God toward His creatures which it contains. . . . The idea of almightiness is present, but it is fully expressed in the word *El*. The word *Shaddai* goes further, and suggests perfect supply and perfect comfort." In the New Testament we find a perfect verse to define El Shaddai: "My grace is sufficient for you, for my power is made perfect in weakness" (2 Corinthians 12:9).

THE LAUGHTER OF SUFFICIENCY

So what did this deficiency of infertility mean to Abraham and Sarah? El Shaddai was about to show up and knock their socks off with little blue booties on ten little toes that belonged to a baby — their very own son.

When Abram was ninety-nine years old, the LORD appeared to him and said, "I am God Almighty; walk before me and be blameless."

"I am God Almighty; walk before me and be blameless" (Genesis 17:1).

God also said to Abraham, "As for Sarai your wife, you are no longer to call her Sarai; her name will be Sarah. I will bless her and will surely give you a son by her. I will bless her so that she will be the mother of nations; kings of peoples will come from her."

Abraham fell facedown; he laughed and said to himself, "Will a son be born to a man a hundred years old? Will Sarah bear a child at the age of ninety?" (GENESIS 17:1, 15–17).

"Where is your wife Sarah?" they asked him. "There, in the tent," he said.

Then the LORD said, "I will surely return to you about this time next year, and Sarah your wife will have a son." Now Sarah was listening at the entrance to the tent, which was behind him. Abraham and Sarah were already old and well advanced in years, and Sarah was past the age of childbearing. So Sarah laughed to herself as she thought, "After I am worn out and my master is old, will I now have this pleasure?"

Then the LORD said to Abraham, "Why did Sarah laugh and say, 'Will I really have a child,

> *now that I am old?' Is anything too hard for the*
> Lord? *I will return to you at the appointed time*
> *next year and Sarah will have a son."*
>
> *Sarah was afraid, so she lied and said, "I did*
> *not laugh." But he said, "Yes, you did laugh."*
>
> (Genesis 18:9–15)

Sarah was barren, old, and well past menopause. Sarah's hot flashes and night sweats only lingered in a distant memory. Estrogen-laden happy cream probably would not have soothed her feelings of inferiority about not being able to give Abraham a son.

Yet, Sarah mustered enough faith to believe that God Almighty was able to overcome her inabilities with His miracle capabilities. *The Message* states, "By faith, barren Sarah was able to become pregnant, old woman as she was at the time, because she believed the One who made a promise would do what he said. That's how it happened that from one man's dead shriveled loins there are now people numbering into the millions" (Hebrews 11:11–12).

Sarah decided to dance with God, although her uterus, so to speak, had two left feet. She laughed. She finally believed. She danced with joy.

We all have this same choice when it comes to believing whether or not God is the El Shaddai in our own lives. Do we believe that He is God Almighty — the All Sufficient One? The decision to believe in His perfect power and perfect comfort allows Him to lead us in a dance that we would be unable to accomplish on our own. But we must be willing to allow Him to lead us through life's disappointments and disabilities.

LEARNING TO LEAN

The award-winning actress Marlee Matlin has a hearing deficiency. At the age of 18 months, Marlee was pronounced profoundly deaf. Although she cannot hear music, Marlee was a contestant on the popular television show *Dancing with the Stars*. It is a contest between several dancing couples — each couple is made up of a professional dancer and a celebrity, but an amateur dancer.

Of course, Marlee Matlin was the amateur. Her dance partner, Fabian Sanchez, was the one who needed to teach her each step of every dance. She had to trust him to teach her to dance without the benefit of her hearing the music. Matlin explained it in a March 24, 2008, *Good Morning America* on abcnews.com article: "Fabian is my music. Fabian, as the man, takes the lead," Matlin said. "He also is my music where I just go with him. I look at him and follow him, as if he's my music, as if he would hear it and try to do it right. It's as simple as that." Matlin followed her teacher. She didn't question — she "listened" and followed his lead.

Her dance instructor, Fabian Sanchez, was the professional dancer. Sanchez described their dance relationship in a March 16, 2008, *Birmingham News* article: "A lot of times, when you have students who can hear the music, they'll try to go at their own beat, whenever they think they're supposed to go, and they won't follow the lead. Marlee has to 100 percent wait for my lead. So she becomes a better follower." Amazing! Matlin trusted Sanchez 100 percent to lead her to victory on the dance floor while millions of people around the world watched.

This sounds like our relationship with God. If we adjust our attitudes toward His capabilities, then we find an enriched

My grace is sufficient for you, for my power is made perfect in weakness (2 Corinthians 12:9).

intimacy in God's arms. I believe as we lean closer into Him for guidance, He whispers in our ears, "My grace is sufficient for you, for my power is made perfect in weakness" (2 Corinthians 12:9).

And this is exactly what happened to baby-deficient Sarah. Although she laughed at the thought of her having a child, eventually she chose to believe in the power of God Almighty. Then the Lord did what He had promised. Sarah became pregnant and gave a son to Abraham in his old age. It all happened at exactly the time God had said it would. And Abraham named his son Isaac, meaning "laughter." Yes, everyone was laughing with joy. Eight days after Isaac was born, Abraham circumcised him as God had commanded. Abraham was one hundred plus years at the time and no longer without an heir. His God was sufficient.

And wizened Sarah declared, "God has brought me laughter! All who hear about this will laugh with me. For who would have dreamed that I would ever have a baby? Yet I have given Abraham a son in his old age!" (Genesis 21:6–7 NLT). This was no retirement party for Sarah and Abraham; instead, it was the beginning of a new lifelong career — parenting. I can imagine Sarah giggling and dancing a Hebrew oompah dance in honor of El Shaddai — the God Almighty who had allowed her deficient womb to bring forth a bouncing baby boy — Isaac — Laughter!

However, although El Shaddai had been more than sufficient in Sarah's life, old insecurities crept into Sarah's joy on the day that she weaned Isaac. She was suddenly filled with inadequacy and jealousy when she spotted Ishmael poking fun at her little boy. The party turned from weaning from Momma's milk to sour milk thoughts.

> *The child grew and was weaned, and on the day Isaac was weaned Abraham held a great feast. But Sarah saw that the son whom Hagar the Egyptian had borne to Abraham was mocking, and she said to Abraham, "Get rid of that slave woman and her son, for that slave woman's son will never share in the inheritance with my son Isaac"* (GENESIS 21:8–10).

TOPSY-TURVY

I always wondered how her joy could turn to such bitter outrage within moments. Yet I have experienced the same reversal of emotions. The flip-flop sentiments usually have nothing to do with reality, but memories hidden deep within my mind still have the power to make me feel inadequate even while I dance in the arms of God Almighty — the All Sufficient One.

For example, like Sarah, my topsy-turvy emotions surfaced recently at a wedding I attended. I was dancing with my husband, Mark, and attempting to follow his lead. He whispered gently, "Count the beats." Suddenly I was awash with my two-left-feet amusia.

Immediately, an ugly memory surfaced. "Count the steps!" my father said as he jerked me. I could smell the sour whiskey on his breath as he yanked me back and forth. He swore. "Can't you hear the music?" he asked as my feet faltered stupidly.

I tried to follow the rhythm and his feet — but could not. My father looked at me in disgust and then shoved me away. He reached out, grabbed my 15-year-old girlfriend, and began to boogie drunkenly with her across the glossy linoleum kitchen floor.

The wedding gaiety dissipated for me, just as the celebration of weaning "Laughter" evaporated like Sarah's milk. Memories — memories I will save for our next dance lesson with our God.

As we celebrate our two left feet — our inadequacies — our God Almighty desires for us to lean into Him with belief because He is El Shaddai — the All Sufficient One. Sarah chose to dance with El Shaddai. Although she laughed at first, she decided to believe He could do what He said He could do. Sarah put aside her deficiency to allow His sufficiency to lead her to the path of motherhood. She knew that God Almighty was enough, is enough, and will always be enough.

Me too. I know that despite my lack of proficiency in any task, if God Almighty–the All Sufficient One — wills it for me, He will lead me in the perfect divine cadence to accomplish it.

Ah, I hear the accordion . . . *oompah-pah oompah-pah.*

Dance Lesson

What type of "deficiency" do you feel you have?

Read 2 Corinthians 12:7–10.

What encouragement does this passage of Scripture reveal about your own insufficiencies?

Is it possible to delight in our own weaknesses? Why or why not?

Fill in your name in the blanks below.
For when _____ is weak, then El Shaddai
makes _____ strong.

Read Philippians 4:13.

How does this correlate with 2 Corinthians 4:7–10?

List areas in your life where you need God Almighty's strength and sufficiency.

Advanced Dance Lesson

Read Acts 3:1–10.

List the probable needs of the beggar.

What didn't Peter have to give to the beggar?

What did he give to the crippled man?

List all the activities of the man listed in verse 8.

What occurred in verse 9? How does this correlate with 2 Corinthians 12:7–10?

Ask God Almighty to give you strength in your area of need. Pray that others will recognize where this new strength comes from and will turn their hearts toward Jesus Christ.

Two Left Feet Journal Page

Jot down your thoughts about God Almighty and His sufficiency in your life.

~~~~~~

~~~~~~

~~~~~~

~~~~~~

~~~~~~

~~~~~~

~~~~~~

~~~~~~

~~~~~~

~~~~~~

~~~~~~

~~~~~~

~~~~~~

~~~~~~

~~~~~~

~~~~~~

~~~~~~

~~~~~~

~~~~~~

Hebrew name: EL SHADDAI

Definition:
THE ALL SUFFICIENT ONE

Modern translations: GOD
ALMIGHTY OR THE
STRONG GOD

When planning a party, provide plenty of seating for those who do not want to participate in planned events. Offer alternate activities to enhance the success of your event. A good hostess will attempt to provide opportunities for social interaction for a wide variety of guests. Here is a list of ideas.

- Dancing
- Swimming
- Croquet
- Board games
- Karaoke
- Quiet places for chatting

Memories Reframed

"Mom, *please* give me the $50 for the prom photos. I never want to forget my senior prom!" my son begged.

Ten years later.

"Mom, I can't believe you kept all those photos from my high school prom. Just tear them up and get rid of them!" my son said.

Photos are memories on hard copy. I enjoy looking back at my kids' pictures and reliving those occasions that are forever past. However, my son reacts differently. The photos cause him to relive those adolescent years he would rather forget.

Usually, photographs remind me of times in my life that I want to remember. I have those "Kodak moments" that I want to recall. I reminisce with the prom pictures, wedding albums, and baby books. Time reverses to the paper-recorded moment I clutch in my hands.

Stephanie, one of my daughters-in-law, goes a step further to keep her memories alive. She organizes the photographs to give them more significance. She scrapbooks them with decorative scissor cuts and archival acid-free paper, and she embellishes them with clever phrases. They are precious pictures bound together as a collection of life.

However, what about those memories I do not want to recall? Of course, I can throw away an actual paper photograph. But what about those pictures of life that pop into my thoughts unbidden? What about those regrettable mistakes, sorrowful incidents, and haunting words that flash through my thoughts without invitation? Something triggers the movie in my mind, the flashbacks that begin to splay in my thoughts in living color. The sin scenes, again. I wish I could toss them into a paper shredder and be done with them forever — irretrievable, disposed of, and forgotten. But unless I develop dementia or Alzheimer's, these memories will stay tucked in the film vault of my mind.

A FIST FULL OF ANGER

It happened when I was in my 20s. Life didn't seem to be going as I had planned. Who was this man I had married? Where did Prince Charming run off to? Why weren't my children perfect? Why was my life stuck in the land of boredom?

In my search for a "perfect life," I began to bargain with God. "I will do that, if You do this." I wanted the Lord to be a genie in a bottle. My wishes, my commands, were there for Him to fulfill. God didn't agree with my plans. He responded with silence. My temper tantrums grew larger. My demands became more insistent. He still didn't react. Then one day, I had had it with the delays. I would show God. I literally stomped my feet on the linoleum floor, lifted my fist at God, and shook it in His holy face. I said, "I am done with You. I'll work out my own life." I walked away into a seven-year desert experience of sin, which ended in divorce, single parenthood, and a desperate struggle to survive financially.

REGRETS RECALL

Over the years, I was held back from a deeper relationship with God by these past regrets in my life — the intentional sin of acting out against God and spewing such hateful words with a purposeful aim. I lament so many of my past behaviors. I reason they must influence how the Lord thinks about me — how He loves me. Because of my past, God wouldn't want to dance with me.

Now, intellectually and theologically, I know this isn't true, but my heart holds me back. My feelings tell me differently. I think, *How could God want to dance with me when He knows what I have done in the past? I wouldn't choose to dance with me.*

Thankfully, in reality my feelings do not affect God's love for me or His desire to woo me into a deeper intimacy with Him. I am grateful for the Bible stories of people who committed horrible sins, but still God came and asked them to follow Him, regardless of their past mistakes.

For example, Moses, who led the Israelites out of the bondage of Egypt to the threshold of God's Promised Land, carried a dark secret that he didn't want exposed — murder. In today's culture, he would be considered a "person of interest" in a homicide investigation. He knew it and fled into a remote foreign desert. He tried to hide from everyone, even God. Here's how Scripture describes Moses's crime.

> One day, after Moses had grown up, he went out to where his own people were and watched them at their hard labor. He saw an Egyptian beating a Hebrew, one of his own people. Glancing this way

and that and seeing no one, he killed the Egyptian and hid him in the sand. The next day he went out and saw two Hebrews fighting. He asked the one in the wrong, "Why are you hitting your fellow Hebrew?"

The man said, "Who made you ruler and judge over us? Are you thinking of killing me as you killed the Egyptian?" Then Moses was afraid and thought, "What I did must have become known."

When Pharaoh heard of this, he tried to kill Moses, but Moses fled from Pharaoh and went to live in Midian, where he sat down by a well (EXODUS 2:11–16).

I can relate to fleeing from the crime scene. When I divorced my first husband and walked away in anger at God, I thought I could hide too. I pocketed my faith in a locket of denial and kept it hidden from everyone.

I remember a time when my new husband, Mark, happened to mention to a few of his colleagues that I had been on a missions trip to Jamaica as a teen. I flew into a rage of embarrassment. My anger flared at Mark, and I saw a look of bewilderment cross his face. He couldn't understand why I was so ashamed of my trip.

I wanted to bury my relationship with the Lord — forever. I was a criminal in hiding.

Doesn't that sound like Moses? In desert obscurity, dressed as a common shepherd, he fooled everyone but God. God knew Moses's history, and He still wanted Moses to become His premier prophet and the emancipator of the Hebrew people.

Toss out the visual of the Charlton Heston version of Moses. Imagine Moses as a sun-wizened, windblown, 80-year-old man — a fugitive. Picture his dirty calloused feet trekking through sheep dung while he is lost in thought about the distant Hebrew God whom he believed no longer cared about him. Then the Lord — the I AM — shows up to disrupt an ordinary day to ask Moses to reframe his memories and to follow Him again.

Allow me to paraphrase the familiar story.

Suddenly, "Hey, Moses! Come over here by the bush that's on fire. But take off those gnarly sandals first — you are standing on holy ground."

Surprised, Moses thinks, Huh?

God says, "Moe, My man, I want to send you back to Egypt to free My people out of that dictator's hand. Lead them to a new land of promise."

At this point Moses holds no illusions of grandeur of who he was, is, or will become. He says, "Who am I that I should go? I guess You aren't aware that I murdered an Egyptian several years ago. I have been on the lam ever since. It's probably not wise to go back."

God says, "I will go with you."

"But," Moses stammers, "who shall I say sent me?"

God says to Moses, "I AM WHO I AM. This is what you are to say to the Israelites: 'I AM has sent me to you.'"

In addition God said, "Say to the Israelites, 'The Lord, the God of your fathers — the God of Abraham, the God of Isaac and the God of

Jacob — has sent me to you.'" God also said to Moses, "Say to the Israelites, 'This is My name forever, the name by which I am to be remembered from generation to generation'" (EXODUS 3:14–15).

> *The LORD . . . "This is my name forever, the name by which I am to be remembered from generation to generation" (Exodus 3:15).*

I AM — JEHOVAH — THE LORD

This name of God, I AM, is often translated in English as LORD. In the ancient Hebrew language, it was *Yahweh*, or Jehovah, as it is more commonly known to us. It was to the ancient Hebrews, and to us, a name that reflects the personal relationship that God desires to have with us. Herbert Stevenson, in *Titles of the Triune God*, explains: "*Jehovah* was His covenant name. It contained within itself the pledge of all that He had promised to do for them and be to them. They were His people, and He their God. They were to know Him in a personal, covenant relationship."

So how does the Lord convince Moses to disregard those old memories and start to dance again? It's important that we understand what the name, I AM, means to us in an English translation. In general, scholars believe that the name renders as "I am, was, and will be." Several other names of the Lord that emphasize the same timeless nature of the name the LORD are:

- The Eternal God (Genesis 21:33)
- The Everlasting God (Isaiah 40:28)

- The Alpha and Omega (Revelation 1:8)
- The Beginning and the End (Revelation 21:6)

We remember and often regret the past, forget to live in the present, and worry about the future. However, here is the difference between our human nature and the LORD's eternal nature. He lives in our pasts, our presents, and our futures.

And graciously, the LORD, or *Yahweh,* has given us several promises to help us reframe our regrets. After He wooed me back from my own sinful trek in the desert, I clutched to three precepts in Scripture. These precepts helped me to reframe my thoughts and my actions and allowed God to lead me into a new dance of the future.

REFRAMED — THE PAST

The first precept was this. While I might dwell in my past mistakes and regrets, the LORD does not. He transcends my past. Isaiah 43:18–19 encourages me. The LORD says, "Forget the former things; do not dwell on the past. See, I am doing a new thing! Now it springs up; do you not perceive it? I am making a way in the desert and streams in the wasteland" (Isaiah 43:18–19). As He did with Moses, God invited me to step out of the wasteland of torn-up memories and reframe them with a new point of reference — His.

He calls me to dance, in spite of my regrets. Moses's mistakes were monumental and life changing — so were mine. And yours probably are too. Yet, I AM asks us not to dwell on them. He has a plan to reframe the old missteps. This new opportunity requires us to have unshackled feet — not regrets clanking behind us like the chains of Marley's ghost from Charles Dickens's *A Christmas Carol.*

NEW PLANS

The second precept is that the Lord has plans for our lives. He assures us with, "'For I know the plans I have for you,' declares the LORD, 'plans to prosper you and not to harm you, plans to give you hope and a future'" (Jeremiah 29:11). *A hope and a future.* I doubt Moses could have ever dreamed what his future would hold, once the Lord presented Himself in that burning bush. Moses was about to become the most prominent prophet the world has ever known.

STILL CALLED TO DANCE

The third precept I hold to is that my gifting and callings are still with me. Even though Moses had made a colossal error, murder, God still called him. Scripture tells us that Moses "was no ordinary child" (Hebrews 11:23). Neither am I; neither are you. We are special in the eyes of God. Remember El Roi, the God who sees me? We are all His children—specially gifted and called. And for the sake of reference, let me state, "the gifts and the calling of God are irrevocable" (Romans 11:29 NASB).

I was called into ministry at a Christian youth camp in northern Utah when I was 17 years old. I was so excited and committed. Was I ready at 17? No. Was Moses ready at age 40? Obviously not, but did Moses's act of violence or my slide into the pit of sin revoke the gift and callings the LORD had placed in our lives? No. It hasn't in your life either. Sin in our lives puts the calling on hold until we repent; then our gracious I AM forgives and proceeds to renew our calling. It may look different, but it will still be God's plan to give us a hope and future with His irrevocable gifts and callings.

For myself, I remember the night I felt that I might still have the privilege of serving God in some type of ministry. I filled the bathtub and slid into it, reflecting on how it seemed God was calling me to lead a high school girls' small group in my home. I plunged deeper in the hot water and excitement bubbled up as ideas blossomed like water lilies.

Then, without invitation, my memory resurrected the images of past sins. Sorrow engulfed me. I felt as if a heavy weight was placed on my chest — I couldn't breathe. Tears of grief dripped into the water. The salty tears dissolved into the clear water. Then it happened — the recognition of the similarity between my tears and my sins. My sins had disappeared into God's love. His grace had covered my sins and now washed me clean. I was free to step out into a new clean life of ministry. Gratitude flooded me.

Yet, the Lord's renewed call to ministry required a response. Determination to never fall back into a desert of sin sprang up like a spring of water. I sat straight up against the porcelain back of the tub and now tears of resolve fell into the water. I prayed, "Lord, do not ever let me stray like that again. I love You. Please take my life if I ever begin to drift in that direction of intentional sin again."

Thankfully, God's grace and my sincere sorrow made an indelible change in my life. It points to the truth of what the Apostle Paul said, "God can use sorrow in our lives to help us turn away from sin and seek salvation. We will never regret that kind of sorrow" (2 Corinthians 7:10 NLT).

Although God doesn't recall our sins, He allows them to be scrapbooked in our minds, so we will experience godly sorrow and turn toward the LORD's arms of love and encouragement.

God can use sorrow in our lives to help us turn away from sin and seek salvation. We will never regret that kind of sorrow (2 Corinthians 7:10 NLT).

On the other hand, we don't always refuse to dance because of the old regrets. We may acknowledge that God has reframed them. But we may choose not to dance because we're too comfortable in the dance steps that we know and we don't want to learn the new dance He wants to teach us. We say, "LORD, my I AM, thanks for reframing those old regrets and making them bearable to live with each day. And thanks for asking me to dance with You. But I want to dance *this* familiar dance forever."

Yet, He calls to us and states, "I AM." Then He whispers into our spirits, "Come, I have surprise for you, My child—a new dance dress."

Dance Lesson

Read Exodus 1 to 2:1–11 and Exodus 32:19.

What additional information is given in the following verses?

Acts 7:20:

Acts 7:22:

Acts 7:23–25:

Acts 7:35–36:

After reading the above verses, write down how we can see the
LORD — I AM — all the way throughout the life of Moses.

Advanced Dance Lesson

Read 2 Samuel 11:1–24.

Briefly describe the events.

Read Psalm 51.

What emotions does David display?

Read 1 Samuel 13:13–14 and Acts 13:22.

What similar statements are made in these two passages?

Whom is God speaking about when He describes "a man after my own heart"?

How can you explain this statement in light of 2 Samuel 11 and Psalm 51?

Memories Reframed Journal Page

Jot down your thoughts about the Lord and the memories in your life that need to be reframed.

~~~~~~

~~~~~~

~~~~~~

~~~~~~

~~~~~~

~~~~~~

~~~~~~

~~~~~~

~~~~~~

~~~~~~

~~~~~~

~~~~~~

~~~~~~

~~~~~~

~~~~~~

~~~~~~

~~~~~~

~~~~~~

~~~~~~

~~~~~~

~~~~~~

~~~~~~

~~~~~~

~~~~~~

Hebrew name: YAHWEH
(JEHOVAH)

Definition: I AM WHO I AM

Modern translation:
THE LORD

Keep the memories of your special event. Photograph or video the guests and special activities. Purchase specialty frames that reflect the event. Or if you enjoy scrapbooking, create a unique scrapbook of the occasion.

- Purchase inexpensive disposable cameras to place on tables for the guests to use throughout the event.
- Delegate one or two people to take pictures and/or video the event.
- Hire a professional photographer/videographer.
- Rent a photo booth for lasting memories and allow the guests to keep a copy.

Dancing Dresses

I hoped my prom dress would slip down easily. I borrowed the dress and it felt snug. The floor-length, tulip yellow satin hung in folds to the tops of my matching open-toed high heels. A flowery bow tied over the left shoulder helped "support" the bodice of the gown. My stepmother cinched the bow tightly in fear that as I danced, the silky bodice might slip to my waist. (Little did she know I was hoping my new boyfriend would untie the knot and help it slide to the floorboard of his truck.)

Although I had accepted the invitation to dance with Jesus Christ at the age of 15, I didn't fully understand the commitment. I still desired the attention of male eyes. And usually, some type of "interesting" apparel accomplished that. Plus, a bit of musky cologne and some heavy makeup would usually draw a second look.

NOT A CLUE

I laugh to think of the first time a godly woman at church told me gently that my skirts were too short to be kneeling in prayer. Shocked, I immediately changed my wardrobe to long gypsy skirts, but I made sure the halter tops still clung to my small waist and accentuated my other assets. Honestly, I just didn't understand the righteous part of being a believer in a holy God.

Thankfully, the Bible provides us with examples of men and women who loved God, but didn't have a clue about righteous behavior either. Many times their actions reflected blatant rebellion against the ordinances of God. Sometimes they lacked biblical knowledge. Or, it was a combination of ignorance and a rebellious decision to do what they deemed the best conduct in a particular situation. In today's culture we would say, "The end justifies the means." My favorite example of this type of skewed thinking is Esther.

Esther was a nice, young, beautiful Jewish girl. Orphaned as a young child, she was raised by her cousin Mordecai. Because of her Hebrew heritage, she lived on the wrong side of social acceptance. The Jewish people had been exiled from their homeland of Israel into captivity in the foreign nation of Babylon. Esther, as we would say, was a girl from the wrong side of the tracks, but she had one thing going for her — she was gorgeous. Let me start from the beginning of the story.

A BIG PARTY

Esther lived in ancient Babylon, which would have been located about 50 miles south of modern Baghdad in Iraq. Babylon was a wealthy, hedonistic empire. The king of Babylon, Xerxes, loved to feast, drink, and show off his treasures. Xerxes decided to throw a big party. The Book of Esther describes it this way: "The celebration lasted six months — a tremendous display of the opulent wealth and glory of his empire" (1:4 NLT). One of his most prized possessions was his beautiful queen — Vashti. Xerxes wanted to show off her good looks. So:

On the seventh day, when King Xerxes was in high spirits from wine, he commanded the seven eunuchs who served him ... to bring before him Queen Vashti, wearing her royal crown, in order to display her beauty to the people and nobles, for she was lovely to look at. But when the attendants delivered the king's command, Queen Vashti refused to come. Then the king became furious and burned with anger (ESTHER 1:10–12).

We do not know why Queen Vashti refused. However, let's give her the benefit of the doubt. The king had been partying for six months, and on this night Xerxes "was in high spirits from wine." Perhaps the complete command was, "Vashti, get to my banquet. Wear your crown — *only* your crown. I want my guys to see you — *all* of you." Whatever the reason, the queen would not obey the command. And the king was not used to being refused — for any reason. Most likely enraged by embarrassment, he banished Vashti from his presence — forever.

He then began a search for a new queen. He plucked beautiful virgin girls from their homes (without permission) to be brought to the palace and prepared for his assessment. Enter Esther.

Mordecai had a cousin named Hadassah, whom he had brought up because she had neither father nor mother. This girl, who was also known as Esther, was lovely in form and features, and Mordecai had taken her as his own daughter when her father and mother died.

> *When the king's order and edict had been proclaimed, many girls were brought to the citadel of Susa and put under the care of Hegai. Esther also was taken to the king's palace and entrusted to Hegai, who had charge of the harem. . . .*
>
> *When the turn came for Esther . . . Esther won the favor of everyone who saw her. She was taken to King Xerxes in the royal residence in the tenth month, the month of Tebeth, in the seventh year of his reign. . . . Now the king was attracted to Esther more than to any of the other women, and she won his favor and approval more than any of the other virgins. So he set a royal crown on her head and made her queen instead of Vashti* (ESTHER 2:7–8, 15–17).

CHOICES

So what does Esther have to do with a party dress of righteousness? I believe Esther, as I did, held little knowledge of what God required in regard to godly behavior. Esther had a choice. It would seem that Esther went willingly before the king, knowing that she would more than likely lose her virginity and probably never see the king again after the one night. Girls were paraded before him like a large box of Valentine chocolates. He could taste and consume what he desired; those he disliked were ruined and rejected.

Again, Esther submitted to an expected standard of behavior. She could have refused (and probably been killed). Esther, at the time, lacked the courage of the former pagan queen, Vashti. Esther chose to go along with the ungodliness of Babylon culture. Now, those of you who know this story are probably crying out, "Heresy! Esther was a godly woman. She put her life at risk."

Yes, she did — finally. After being reprimanded by Mordecai, Esther made the decision to risk her own position and possibly her life in an attempt to help all the other Jews. She did rescue her people from an evil man, Haman, who was out to annihilate all Jews. But she did not stand up for her Jewish beliefs in the beginning. She was dolled up and looked great on the outside, but Esther, at least in the beginning, did not possess a courageous righteousness.

PARTY DRESSES

My point is that "our very best party dresses" do not translate into righteousness. I wanted my yellow dress to entice my Prince Charming for one prom night of "love." Esther "endured" 12 months of beauty treatments, so she could sashay into the king's arms for a one-night quickie. I was a young Christian believer. She was a young Jewish virgin. We chose not to come to our dances in righteous and innocent attire.

Thankfully, God does not rely on our human knowledge or strength to produce righteousness in us. He knows what our party dresses look like. The prophet Isaiah wrote an apt description: "All of us have become like one who is unclean, and all our righteous acts are like filthy rags" (Isaiah 64:6). Righteousness is not just goodness. It is not even the *desire* to do right. It is *always* doing what God says is right. Righteous living is *completely* living by His holy standards, which is an impossibility for us — "There is none righteous, no, not one" (Romans 3:10 KJV).

JEHOVAH-TSIDKENU — WHO?

Gratefully, our God dresses us in His own righteousness. The tearful prophet Jeremiah wrote, "And this is his name: 'The LORD Is Our Righteousness'" (Jeremiah 23:6 NLT). In Hebrew it would be *Jehovah-tsidkenu* (in older Bible versions). This tongue twister is pronounced *Je hoh'vuh-tssiddkee' nyoo*. Let's just stick with the Lord (Is) Our Righteousness.

When we accept the invitation to dance with the Lord God, He clothes us in His very best party attire—the holy blood of Jesus Christ. The Bible tells the modern believer:

And this is his name: "The Lord Is Our Righteousness" (Jeremiah 23:6 NLT).

> *For our sake He made Christ [virtually] to be sin Who knew no sin, so that in and through Him we might become [endued with, viewed as being in, and examples of] the righteousness of God [what we ought to be, approved and acceptable and in right relationship with Him, by His goodness]* (2 CORINTHIANS 5:21 AMP).

> *Namely, the righteousness of God which comes by believing with personal trust and confident reliance on Jesus Christ (the Messiah). [And it is meant] for all who believe. For there is no distinction* (ROMANS 3:22 AMP).

Of course, the Lord Our Righteousness, Jehovah-tsidkenu, still desires for us to strive for righteous behavior. But because He is the perfect parent, He knows that we can't dress ourselves very well.

DRESSED TO THE NINES

I have a running joke with my oldest son that I could blackmail him with a photo we took of him the first day of sixth grade. My independent, strong-willed son had dressed himself for the first day of middle school. He thought he looked great — dressed to the nines. It was so awful, he wouldn't have been considered dressed to the sixes, let alone the nines. Let me explain.

Standing for his back-to-school photo, he has a bright smile and six fingers held high to indicate sixth grade. My son's white T-shirt boasts a blue decal of his favorite sports team. He has on long yellow and orange Hawaiian-print surfing shorts. They hang to the middle of his calves. His long white athletic socks peek over the top of his red high-top tennis shoes. Honestly, the picture could make the rounds as the next forwarded email with the subject line, "Smile for Today."

Now his response to my teasing is, "That's OK. You should never have allowed me out of the house dressed like that, let alone sent me to my first day of middle school. Call the papers. They will call child protection services on you — there's no statute of limitations on child embarrassment." We burst out laughing together. Thankfully, the Father takes full responsibility for dressing His children. He dresses them beautifully and with respect. Indeed, He dresses us to the nines in party dresses of righteousness.

MASQUERADE

Often when we dress ourselves, we pretend to be something that we are not. Heaven only knows what my son thought he was masquerading as on the first day of sixth grade. For myself I have costumed myself in my "power suit," which entails a navy skirt and blazer, bright red blouse, high-heeled shoes, and briefcase. It tells the world not to mess with me — I am in charge of my destiny. Or, I have my "Christian" wardrobe. I carry a Bible with a needlepoint cover. I clothe myself in softer colors, higher necklines, longer skirts, and flat shoes. I feel these grant me a better perception of who I think I should be as a Christian woman. Who am I kidding? No one.

Allow me to go back to Esther. She masqueraded too. She hid her Jewish background from the king's court. "Esther had not revealed her nationality and family background, because Mordecai had forbidden her to do so" (Esther 2:10).

But her identity could not be hidden forever. Her "happily-ever-after life" suddenly changed. A wicked man, Haman, set out to destroy all the Jews. Esther's cousin Mordecai suddenly went from telling her to hide her nationality to demanding that she rescue her relatives — the Jews. He said:

> *"Do not think that because you are in the king's house you alone of all the Jews will escape. For if you remain silent at this time, relief and deliverance for the Jews will arise from another place, but you and your father's family will perish. And who knows but that you have come to royal position for such a time as this?"* (ESTHER 4:13–14).

In other words, "Stop masquerading and help us!" Eventually, Esther agreed and said her famous words, "And if I perish, I perish" (Esther 4:16). Could this crisis have been avoided if in the beginning Esther had not masked her identity? Perhaps, the king would have rejected Esther, or maybe he would have still been so enamored with Esther that she still would have become the queen. Perhaps wicked Haman would not have dared to initiate the plot to kill the Jews. We can only guess.

However, sweet, young, innocent Esther could have declared the truth and refused to go into the king and lose her innocence from the beginning. She could have refused by declaring righteous obedience to her God was more important than her life. "If I perish, I perish."

Thankfully, the Lord Our Righteousness understands that we tend to masquerade through life. Whether we are Old Testament girls or New Testament believers, He knows our pretenses. Again, the Bible says, "We are all infected and impure with sin. When we proudly display our righteous deeds, we find they are but filthy rags" (Isaiah 64:6 NLT). Yet, He cleans us up: "Cleanse me with hyssop, and I will be clean; wash me, and I will be whiter than snow" (Psalm 51:7). And He gives us a dress of righteousness: "And to her was granted that she should be arrayed in fine linen, clean and white: for the fine linen is the righteousness of saints" (Revelation 19:8 KJV). That's our God! He is a God who provides His dance partners beautiful linen dresses of righteousness. No need to worry about making sure the straps stay tied. No masquerade mask required with this Beau who loves to dance with us despite our insecurities and dirty self-righteous rags. When He asks us to dance, He provides the attire.

Not only does the Lord Our Righteousness clothe us in dancing dresses, He provides us with guardians—angelic protection because He is the God of the Angel Armies too.

Cleanse me with hyssop, and I will be clean; wash me, and I will be whiter than snow (Psalm 51:7).

Dance Lesson

Do you ever attempt to masquerade as someone you're not? If yes, why? (fear, pride, desire).

Read Esther 8:1–11.

When Esther revealed her actual identity, what happened?

In your opinion, do you think Esther was wise to hide her nationality at Mordecai's bidding? Why or why not?

How did Jehovah-tsidkenu rescue Esther and Mordecai from their predicament?

Is there a masquerade in your life that you would like to remove and replace with God's righteousness?

Let's ask our Lord-tsidkenu for a party dress of righteousness:

Lord God, I possess no righteousness of my own. My righteousness is a masquerade. It is just filthy rags hiding behind a façade of goodness. Please come and dress me in Your fine linen of Christ's righteousness. Clothe me with goodness, so that I might be acceptable to You and feel beautiful inside and out. I long to be beautiful in Your eyes. I ask this in Your name, Jehovah-tsidkenu, my righteousness, amen.

Advanced Dance Lesson

Write out Jeremiah 23:6*b* and 33:16*b*.

Read 1 Corinthians 1:26–31.

Do you consider yourself to be wise, influential, or of noble birth? If yes, explain.

How does the Lord Our Righteousness apply to 1 Corinthians 1:30?

What instruction does verse 31 give?

How can you boast in Jehovah-tsidkenu?

Using Psalm 143:1–2, 10–11 for inspiration, write a closing prayer to Jehovah-tsidkenu, the Lord Our Righteousness.

Dancing Dresses Journal Page

Jot down your thoughts about the Lord Our Righteousness and
His desire to clothe you in His righteousness.

~~~~~~
~~~~~~
~~~~~~
~~~~~~
~~~~~~
~~~~~~
~~~~~~
~~~~~~
~~~~~~
~~~~~~
~~~~~~
~~~~~~
~~~~~~
~~~~~~
~~~~~~
~~~~~~
~~~~~~
~~~~~~
~~~~~~
~~~~~~

Hebrew name: JEHOVAH-TSIDKENU

Definition: THE LORD IS OUR RIGHTEOUSNESS

Modern name: THE LORD OUR RIGHTEOUSNESS

Party Attire Definitions

Black Tie or Formal: A black tie or formal event calls for the dressiest of attire. Men wear tuxedos. Women wear cocktail or long dresses that are elegant and formal.

Semiformal: Long dresses or tuxedos are not required. However, for a woman the proper attire is a cocktail dress or a dressy suit. For the man, a dark suit is appropriate.

Business Formal: For the man, this is the same as semiformal. For the woman, a tailored dressy suit or a nice dress is suggested.

Informal or Dressy Casual: A sports coat for the man is appropriate. For the woman, a dress or suit is suggested.

Casual: Depending on the event location, almost anything within good taste will do.

Theme Party: Consider the holiday or theme that the party is planned around. Christmas parties suggest sparkly sweaters, red tops with black skirts, etc. Beach picnic events require a swimsuit and cover-up. For a backyard barbeque, appropriate dress would be jeans, shorts, and T-shirts.

Fox-trot Escorts

Whatever you do, don't hit the brakes on the slick roads," my dad said.

At 16 and a new driver, I didn't heed his instruction. I knew how to drive. Hadn't I taken driver's education for three months?

So, my best friend and I headed off to the high school. My cocky attitude coaxed the gas pedal closer to the floorboard. I held the wheel with one palm. I felt self-assured in my ability, but the icy road decided to deflate my youthful arrogance. The ice on asphalt threatened me as my orange Volkswagen slid a bit. I chose to ignore the warning. Suddenly, we began to glide like a marble on a tile floor. I slammed on the brakes, which caused me to lose control. We slid downhill, spinning sideways, and picking up speed. We were headed for the left side of a large red Cadillac sedan.

I had no training in the subject of prayer and faith. All I thought to do was squeak out, "Jesus, Jesus!"

FOX-TROT ESCORT 1

Here's what I assume happened. The car continued to skid toward the ruby monster. My car spun again. We braced ourselves for impact when my tidbit car stopped suddenly. Shocked, I looked at my friend. Her mouth agape, she stared back. We opened the doors cautiously and stepped gingerly onto the icy road. We crept forward toward the front bumper of our vehicle. We discovered we could not have slid a piece of paper between the two cars, but we didn't smash into the sedan. Surely, an unseen servant of my heavenly Father prevented my orange Beetle from colliding with the burgundy Cadillac and making my earthly father see red.

I was a new believer — no more than a couple of months old in my dance of faith. I didn't know what to expect when I cried, "Jesus! Jesus!" I knew I needed help — fast. Although I was in no physical danger, my father would have been furious and I would have been humiliated. But God Almighty came to my rescue. He proved His sovereignty to an inexperienced driver and immature believer. God responded to this foolish pip-squeak's prayer, I believe, by sending an angel. That frosty winter day, He revealed Himself to me as the Lord Almighty — God of the Angel Armies.

I am not a theologian on angels, but I do believe in their existence — because the Bible tells me so. Billy Graham aptly expresses in *Angels*: "I am convinced that these heavenly beings exist and they provide unseen aid on our behalf. . . . I do not believe in angels because I have ever seen one — because I haven't. I believe in angels because the Bible says there are angels; and I believe the Bible to be the true Word of God."

I believe that God sent an angel to provide unseen aid for me that day on my way to high school. A passage of Scripture that supports the concept of angels as our unseen protectors is the story of the prophet Elisha who had angered the pagan king of Aram, a neighboring nation of Israel. When the king hunted down and located Elisha, he sent troops with chariots to do away with the prophet. A servant of Elisha spotted the opposing army encamped around them. He ran back to his master, Elisha, and with a woeful cry asked, "Oh, my lord, what shall we do?"

Elisha didn't even go out to look. He just replied with, "Don't be afraid. Those who are with us are more than those who are with them." Then Elisha prayed. "O LORD, open his eyes so he may see." The Bible says, "Then the LORD opened the servant's eyes, and he looked and saw the hills full of horses and chariots of fire all around Elisha" (2 Kings 6:16–17). Billy Graham remarks, in *Angels*, on these verses, "This passage has been one of the great assurances and comforts to me in my ministry." I agree with Graham that it is a comfort to know that although we might not see them, angels are about.

So, on that note, I *think* I have experienced the intervention of angels in my life — probably three times. Strangely, they all involved me as a driver of my own vehicle. (Do you think that might say something about my driving?) And, let me make it perfectly clear that I am not a person who believes that a guardian angel is at my beck and call.

However, I do believe that my God is *Jehovah-sabaoth* [SABB-aa-oath], which translates from the Hebrew as the "Lord of Hosts" or the "Lord Almighty." My favorite modern translation for this powerful name is in *The Message* — God of the Angel Armies. My heart races at the thought that my dance partner is *the* God of armies of angels who dash to do His will. They work on our behalf because they desire to see the will of God fulfilled in our lives. They serve out of their own inexhaustible love for the Lord Almighty and His love for us.

So if our God is the Lord of the angels, who are these celestial beings? The Bible often depicts them as messengers of God sent to protect us. Psalm 91:11 says, "For he will command his angels concerning you to guard you in all your ways." Or, in the Book of Hebrews, "But angels are only servants. They are spirits sent from God to care for those who will receive salvation" (1:14 NLT).

I would describe angels as the Lord's Fox-trot Escorts. These guardians are servants of God who serve His purposes only. They are sent to relay a message, to protect, to guard, and to guide us. So, why do I reference them as the fox-trot escorts? Because the steps of the fox-trot dance are intricate and hazardous for even the best of dancers. Let me explain the fox-trot dance.

THE FOX-TROT

We do not know how or when angels were created. But we do know when and where the fox-trot originated. It was initiated in the summer of 1914 in New York City. Its choreographer was a vaudeville entertainer, Harry Fox, who inserted the dance as part of his act. He would trot steps to ragtime music and people began to call it Fox's Trot. It became a cultural phenomenon, partly because of the combination of quick and slow steps that replaced the familiar and boring one- or two-step dances. The fox-trot's variety added the thrill of difficulty and a bit of danger of twisting an ankle. The fox-trot hooked dancers with its complexity and penchant for missteps.

Angels could be our fox-trot escorts. The God of the Angel Armies may send out these celestial servants to rescue us when we are in an "out of our control" situation. The fox-trot escorts can protect us as we stumble through the misguided steps of life. I think Scripture illustrates at least four types of angelic activity on earth:

1. To increase our faith in God's sovereignty
2. To protect us from danger when He wills our safety
3. To protect other people from our reckless behavior
4. To send a message by heavenly courier

When the orange Bug did not collide with the Cadillac barge, I learned an aspect of God that I was not fully aware of in my walk of faith — His sovereignty. I saw that God could protect when I made foolish decisions — even when they were deliberate. I realized I served a God who was in complete control of my life — even over my foolish teenage invincibility.

It reminds me of the story in the Bible concerning the disobedient prophet Balaam. The Lord Almighty instructs Balaam not to curse the Israelites. However, a large bribe from the king of Moab had the greedy prophet rethinking things about issuing a curse over the Hebrews. Balaam decides the bribe money would come in handy. So off he rides down the slippery slope of greed and self-assurance to curse God's people.

WHOA, DONKEY!

Suddenly, the beast veers off the path because an angel of God is blocking the path with a sword that flickers in the sun. Balaam beats the donkey. Again — proceed, stop, beat; again — proceed, stop, beat.

Then the profiteer prophet gets a scolding — from the donkey! *The Message* describes it:

> *Then GOD gave speech to the donkey. She said to Balaam: "What have I ever done to you that you have beat me these three times?"*
>
> *Balaam said, "Because you've been playing games with me! If I had a sword I would have killed you by now."*
>
> *The donkey said to Balaam, "Am I not your trusty donkey on whom you've ridden for years right up until now? Have I ever done anything like this to you before? Have I?"*
>
> *He said, "No."*
>
> *Then GOD helped Balaam see what was going on: He saw GOD's angel blocking the way, brandishing a sword. Balaam fell to the ground, his face in the dirt* (NUMBERS 22:28–31).

Balaam probably did a mental head slap — duh! duh! duh!

Yes, the Lord Almighty demonstrated He can and does intervene, sometimes by angels, to show His sovereignty to stubborn Balaam and obstinate Susanne.

I find this interesting. The first time Scripture refers to God as the God of the Angel Armies is in the book of 1 Samuel. The story is of a faithful man, Elkanah, who worships the Lord Almighty. It states, "Every year this man went from his hometown up to Shiloh to worship and offer a sacrifice

Every year this man went from his hometown up to Shiloh to worship and offer a sacrifice to God-of-the-Angel-Armies (1 Samuel 1:3 THE MESSAGE).

to GOD-of-the-Angel-Armies" (1 Samuel 1:3 *The Message*). I think the point of acknowledging God as the Lord Almighty is this: The Lord of angel armies deserved the worship and sacrifice — not the angels. This fact holds true for us today.

FOX-TROT ESCORT 2

I believe the second time I experienced an angelic intervention, I was having a bad day all the way around. The weather stifled my breath like a heavy wet blanket over my face. The humidity and heat made my emotions rise to the boiling point. To make matters worse, I was driving my sullen-faced teenage son around trying to find a tailor to sew patches on his school letter jacket. (In his adolescent opinion, it was the priority of life.)

We drove endlessly looking for the tailor's home. Somehow, we ended up on a long empty road that headed out of the city. I pulled off the road to regroup. Caustic words flowed from my mouth as sweat beaded on my forehead. My son lashed back with teenage "smack talk." In a rage, I threw the car into drive and whipped a U-turn on the supposedly empty road.

In a flash, I saw another vehicle barreling toward us at a high rate of speed. My sight blurred for a moment, as it appeared the car flew toward my driver's side door. Somehow, through the grace of God, it did not hit us. I cannot tell you how it did not, except that I believe that Lord Almighty sent an angel. If my car had been hit, it would have been demolished. I surely would have died and probably my son too. All I can say is, it was not God's purpose for me to die at that time.

I know that someone is reading this and saying, "Why didn't God protect my loved one? Why did he have to die?" I don't know. I can't say why the God of the Angel Armies — the fox-trot escorts — chooses to protect sometimes and not at other times. I could die tomorrow in a car accident, by cancer, or by any other cause. When that time comes, it will be because my purpose in this life has been fulfilled. I find comfort in Acts 13:36, "For when David had served God's purpose in his own generation, he fell asleep; he was buried with his fathers." I know when my dance card is full, God will take me home to be with Him.

DIVINE INTERVENTION 3

A few months ago, I scurried around town completing my errands. Anxious to get home, I headed out of the supermarket parking lot. I glanced right. I looked left and then gunned the car into a right-hand turn. Then right before my eyes, a little boy about the age of eight materialized right in front of me. His chocolate brown eyes widened, and I saw the fear well up in them. I slammed the brakes, and with the intervention of God, I did not run over the child. I felt nausea rise in me, then relief, then utter gratitude because, once again, I had witnessed a miracle.

For myself, I believe I have witnessed the intervention of unseen heavenly hosts in my life three times. However, I have never experienced the angels' primary biblical purpose. The Bible seems to indicate that the angels' chief purpose is to deliver a message from the Lord Almighty. I have not and don't expect to have a message by angelic delivery. But there are several messages delivered to people in the Bible.

- To Mary the mother of Jesus (Luke 1:29–30)
- To ordinary shepherds to announce the birth of Jesus (Luke 2:8–14)

- To demon-free Mary Magdalene after the resurrection of Jesus (Matthew 28:5–8)

When these angelic beings appeared, they usually began the message with the words, "Do not be afraid!" The recipient of the message required reassurance. The messengers were sent with an invitation to learn another dance with difficult dance steps with their partner, the Lord Almighty.

ANGEL ACCURACY

Our culture portrays angels as cute and cuddly cherubs. They supposedly initiate romance. They adorn Valentine cards and boxes of chocolates. Or angels are characterized as genies in a bottle, ready to do the bidding of humans. A December 27, 1993, *Time* article by Nancy Gibbs said, "In their modern incarnation, these mighty messengers and fearless soldiers have been reduced to bite-size beings, easily digested. The terrifying cherubim have become Kewpie-doll cherubs. For those who choke too easily on God and his rules, theologians observe, angels are the handy compromise, all fluff and meringue, kind, nonjudgmental. And they are available to everyone, like aspirin."

These images are polar opposites from how the Bible describes the hosts of heaven. The fox-trot escorts are mighty and mysterious. They are not submissive to our desires or wishes — they are created beings of the Lord of Hosts. They obey and submit to the command of the God of the Armies of Angels *only*. Psalm 103 sums it up:

Praise the LORD, you his angels,
  you mighty ones who do his bidding,
  who obey his word.
Praise the LORD,
  all his heavenly hosts,
  you his servants who do his will (20–21).

Angels do His will and His bidding. God commands any interaction between angels and His children on earth.

In closing, I will allow Billy Graham, from his book *Angels,* to express eloquently his thoughts on angels:

> *Every true believer in Christ should be encouraged and strengthened! . . . They mark our path. They superintend the events of lives and protect the interest of the Lord God, always working to promote His plans to bring about His highest will for us.*

My own experience of those split-second rescues has cemented my belief in angels.

For myself, as I attempt to learn every new step with God, I know I have escorts who watch me through my folly and my faith — who will rescue me if He bids because He is the Lord Almighty, the God of the Angel Armies.

This knowledge of the fox-trot escorts enables me to attempt the more difficult assignments that the God of the Angel Armies might command of me. When the Lord Almighty makes a special request of me — a new challenging step — I will attempt it because I believe that He could send an angel to help.

Dance Lesson

Read the following verses and jot down what you learn about angels.

Hebrews 1:1–13:

Hebrews 1:14:

Matthew 4:7–11:

Luke 15:10:

Psalm 148:2:

Advanced Dance Lesson

Read Acts 12:1–11.

In verse 2, what happened to James?

How did Peter escape prison?

What were Peter's first thoughts?

What did Peter state in verse 11?

Explain your feelings about the different results for James and Peter.

Does Acts 13:36 change your thoughts about the results for James and Peter? Why or why not?

Fox-trot Escorts Journal Page

Jot down your thoughts about the Lord Almighty, God of the Angel Armies.

~~~~~~

~~~~~~

~~~~~~

~~~~~~

~~~~~~

~~~~~~

~~~~~~

~~~~~~

~~~~~~

~~~~~~

~~~~~~

~~~~~~

~~~~~~

~~~~~~

~~~~~~

~~~~~~

~~~~~~

~~~~~~

~~~~~~

~~~~~~

Hebrew name: JEHOVAH-SABAOTH

Definition: LORD OF HOSTS OR LORD OF ANGELS

Modern translations: LORD ALMIGHTY OR GOD OF THE ANGEL ARMIES

The Fox-trot

The fox-trot is a difficult dance to learn. It is quick in 4/4 time. Each measure of music has four separate and distinct beats. The change in steps from slow-slow-quick-quick within the dance creates an interest that follows throughout all the movements. Learning to dance the fox-trot requires patience and lots of practice. Because of the variety of steps, it can be one of the most difficult dances to master.

My head hung in shame as I turned in my resignation. Tears flooded my eyes and spilled out onto my flaming red cheeks. My rueful embarrassment bruised my soul until I almost felt physical pain. I had disobeyed the Lord and this was the end result — humiliation. My pride crumpled like a ballerina with a broken ankle.

The story began like a beautiful ballet when my family began attending a trendy new church. One evening our two teenage sons came home chattering about a new pastor they had heard at a youth group event. My husband and I were accustomed to male grunts for conversation, and now the boys were chattering like a cage full of canaries. We glanced at each other and agreed silently we would have to check out this pastor and his church.

We attended the following Sunday and were smitten too. We enjoyed the music. The teaching satisfied our spirits. The people purposed it to be a friendly and welcoming place. Even the coffee and bagels tasted fresher to us. We decided we were finished with "stale" churches; we wanted to be a part of this congregation. No longer were we going to be church potatoes sitting as bored audience members. No, we were going to serve and be involved. My husband began helping with setup and teardown at the high school where we held our Sunday services. I learned the nursery needed volunteers too. So I began to rock babies in the nursery during one of our services. I also volunteered for administrative tasks in the church office during the week.

Soon pride began to parade around in my thoughts. I wasn't satisfied with my tasks. No longer satisfied with my supporting role in this dance troupe, I wished for a principal part. I wanted to be a prima donna in this cool megachurch. I didn't want a subordinate role as a volunteer. No, I wanted to be in the inner circle—I wanted to be on staff. In time, an opportunity presented itself and I auditioned for the part.

CHOREOGRAPHY GONE AWRY

I sent in my résumé to be the head of the children's department—the Kiddie Kingdom director. No one else wanted any part of this job; my application was the only one submitted to the senior pastor and the elders. I interviewed with the pastor and then we both said spiritually, "Let's pray about it."

I prayed all right. I issued an edict to God: "I want this position! I want to be on staff! I want to be part of the inner circle. I want it!"

In my spirit, I heard the Lord say, *No, this is the wrong part for you. Trust Me.*

"But I want it, want it, want it!"

Again, the soft but insistent voice, *No! This is not to be the ministry I called you to—just wait. Be patient.*

"I don't want to wait," I said.

The next day I called the pastor and said, "If you will have me, I would like to take the position."

"Wonderful! You can start on Tuesday when we have our weekly staff meeting," he said with relief in his voice. "Oh, and don't forget that in two weeks it will be Easter Sunday. We have record attendance, so make sure there are plenty of volunteers to watch the multitude of kids."

The primary role was filled in Kiddie Kingdom. The pastor was relieved. I was thrilled to be on staff, but I felt a slight gnawing anxiety. The Lord was silent.

However, on Wednesday of that week, I proudly pinned on my name badge identifying me as "staff of the cool megachurch." It was blue and white plastic, and it read: *Susanne Scheppmann, Kiddie Kingdom Director*.

MISUSED TITLE

The name I utilize the most when I speak of God is *the Lord*. Or when I pray, it is how I usually address Him. However, many times I do not use it in the correct connotation. Is He actually my Lord? Do I act like it?

The name "Lord" is *Adonai* in the Hebrew language. It is one of the most frequently used titles throughout the entire Bible. The first time we read this name in Scripture is in Genesis 15. "But Abram said, 'O Sovereign LORD, what can you give me since I remain childless and the one who will inherit my estate is Eliezer of Damascus?'" (Genesis 15:2).

Abram addressed God as Adonai, which translates as *Lord* in English. Abram recognized the sovereignty of God in his life. In this name, Adonai or Lord, we recognize God's premier right to rule over us — like the choreographer of a dance recital. However, for myself, I seem to end up tap dancing around the title *Lord*. I want the benefits of Him being God in my life, but I do not always submit to His authority.

Instead, I go about my life doing what I *think* is best. Kay Arthur describes this attitude in her book *Lord, I Want to Know You*. She writes:

> But does what I do matter as long as I acknowledge Him as Lord and tell Him I want His free gift of eternal life? Yes, it does!
>
> Lord is more than a word; it indicates a relationship. The lordship of God means His total possession of me and my total submission to Him as Lord and Master.

TAP DANCING

Tap dancing probably originated in Africa, although the term *tap dance* began in America. Tap dancing has its own type of jargon, such as "stealing steps" and "challenges." Early tap dancers often referred to their trying to outdo each other. Even in old movies, tap dancers often challenged each other with ever-increased speed and difficulty of steps. These dances were often called challenges as dancers attempted to outdance one another. Because of this one-upmanship mentality,

But Abram said, "O Sovereign LORD, what can you give me since I remain childless and the one who will inherit my estate is Eliezer of Damascus?" (Genesis 15:2).

a second definition of tap dance came about. Tap dancing is construed as a deliberate course of action that is intended to rationalize a person's behavior or intended to distract someone else's attention from the real issue. This second definition is what I tend do with the Lord's authority in my life.

Tap dancing around God's authority is an ancient dance.

The crusty old prophet Elijah challenged the Israelites to decide whom they were going to serve and obey: the Adonai who is LORD (*Yahweh*) and God (*Elohim*) or the false god Baal. He went before the tap dancing Hebrews and said, "'How long will you waver between two opinions? If the LORD is God, follow him; but if Baal is God, follow him.' But the people said nothing" (1 Kings 18:21). Frustrated, Elijah determined to prove to them who was the true Lord God.

"How long will you waver between two opinions? If the LORD is God, follow him" (1 Kings 18:21).

It is interesting that when you view the word *waver* in the Hebrew, it can translate in some instances as *dance*. So, in other words, Elijah was asking the Israelites, "How long are you going to tap dance between your opinions of who is the Lord God?"

Elijah calls for sacrifices to be prepared — one for Yahweh, who is Adonai, and one for Baal. He issues the challenge, "'Then you call on the name of your god, and I will call on the name of the LORD [YAHWEH]. The god who answers by fire — he is God.' Then all the people said, 'What you say is good'" (1 Kings 18:24). Of course, Baal was a no-show to the performance. Not even a spark hit his sacrifice. But the Lord God showed up — even after Elijah had poured 12 large jars of water on the bull and wood. The story ends with this dramatic finale:

> *Then the fire of the LORD fell and burned up the sacrifice, the wood, the stones and the soil, and also licked up the water in the trench.*
>
> *When all the people saw this, they fell prostrate and cried, "The LORD — he is God! The LORD — he is God!"* (1 KINGS 18:38–39).

KIDDIE KINGDOM CALAMITY

My title of Kiddie Kingdom director lasted for a short time. Specifically, until the day after Easter Sunday. So, in essence, it was a two-week performance. I was in over my ability. The director of Kiddie Kingdom needed to make sure all volunteer child-care positions were fully staffed according to the state legal requirements. And as the director, I was required to decide on proper curriculum for teaching the children. Included in the job description, which I am sure was in fine print, was the job of keeping all the supplies, such as baby wipes, tissues, and disinfectant ready whenever and wherever needed. And, I was responsible for supplying craft ideas and the supplies for each activity.

There was no children's volunteer list. So I used my husband, my two sons, and anyone I considered a friend. I tried to enlist any person who crossed my path. I begged. I pleaded. I groveled for help. I shopped. I gazed dazedly at children's craft ideas. I loaded my van with baby supplies and anything that appeared capable of being turned into a child's craft project.

After the Wednesday and Sunday services, I left frustrated

and exhausted. I knew I was out of the will of God. I had tap danced around Him and now I was trying to catch my breath in the whirlwind of my own farce. I wrestled with the age-old question: God was my dance partner — but was He my *Lord*?

Was Jesus the Lord of my life? I already knew the answer to my question. No, He was not my Adonai, at least not in the dance of the Kiddie Kingdom director. No, I had not allowed Him to lead me into a dance of His choice. I had gone willfully and disobediently after my own heart's wishes. And the Lord had permitted me to follow my own steps, to stumble and fall into failure.

Then, I read the verses that confirmed the knowledge of my willfulness against Jesus.

> *Jesus said it this way, "You call me 'Master' and 'Lord,' and you do well to say it, for it is true"* (JOHN 13:13 TLB).

> *"Why do you call me, 'Lord, Lord,' and do not do what I say?"* (LUKE 6:46).

No, I had not followed Adonai's command. I was moving in the wrong direction in this ministry. I couldn't find my footing. Obstacles loomed in front of me. I bumbled into the other staff's time and energies as they tried to stay out of my misguided ministry. I realized I had choreographed a ministry path of my own choice. If the Lord had asked me to dance this dance, He would have provided the knowledge and the skills for me to perform it.

My failure was not His fault. I decided to resign from the position.

My husband, mortified with the thought of the embarrassment I would cause myself, said, "I will help you. I will babysit every week." (Sweet thing that he is.) No, I was not going to be a part of the Kiddie Kingdom, but I was going to be obedient to my Lord of lords and King of kings.

I sat at my computer and scripted my resignation letter. Humbly, I attempted to put into words my disobedience and my lack of ability to continue as the director of Kiddie Kingdom.

I learned a powerful lesson from this time of tap dancing out of God's will. Sometimes He allows me to have my own foot-stomping way. He won't take bribes or give in to my pitiful tantrums. He is God — Adonai — the Lord. Moses spoke truth when he declared:

> "GOD, your God, is the God of all gods, he's the Master of all masters, a God immense and powerful and awesome. He doesn't play favorites, takes no bribes"
> (DEUTERONOMY 10:17 THE MESSAGE).

God had called me into ministry, but not children's ministry. My husband and I stayed at "the cool church" until they started a "cool church plant." At that time, we felt the Lord asking us to dance on over to this new dance floor and help them become established. It felt good to be obedient to His will.

Little did I know, I was about to receive a special request from Adonai — my Lord and Master. It was a special request that I began to tap dance away from instead of accepting. I am a great tap dancer, but a poor learner. It wouldn't be long before I needed to decide again whether Adonai was Lord of my life or not.

Dance Lesson

Read 1 Samuel 13.

Who was Saul?

Describe why and what Saul did in verses 7–10.

What question did the prophet Samuel ask Saul? (v. 11).

How did Saul respond in verse 12?

What did Samuel prophesy would be the results of Saul's disobedience?

List the reasons why we often tap dance around the Lord's instructions to us.

Advanced Dance Lesson

Read 1 Samuel 15:7–26.

Describe Saul's disobedience in these verses.

What does verse 17 say happened to Saul in his own eyes?

How does Saul object to Samuel about His disobedience? (vv. 20–21).

Write Samuel's response to Saul in verse 22.

Was God the Lord of Saul's life? Explain.

Is He the Lord of your life? Why or why not?

Tap Dancing Journal Page

Jot down your thoughts about being obedient to the Lord in every area of your life.

~~~~~~

~~~~~~

~~~~~~

~~~~~~

~~~~~~

~~~~~~

~~~~~~

~~~~~~

~~~~~~

~~~~~~

~~~~~~

~~~~~~

~~~~~~

~~~~~~

~~~~~~

~~~~~~

~~~~~~

~~~~~~

~~~~~~

~~~~~~

~~~~~~

Hebrew name: ADONAI

Definition: LORD

Modern translations: LORD, MASTER

Dance Floor Etiquette

Good dance etiquette requires you to follow the dance floor rules of movement. There are two types of dance movements on the floor—either progressive or spot dances. The fox-trot, waltz, and similar styles are progressive. The dancers move around the dance floor in a counterclockwise rotation. A tap dance, rumba, or cha-cha would be considered a spot dance, where the dancers stay within a small area near where they began.

Dance courtesy is the same as that of any other social occasion—use your manners and politeness. And, of course, always apologize when you accidentally bump or step on someone. Do not cut off other dancers as they circle on the floor.

Special Request

I rocked in my favorite chair as I began my morning quiet time. I lounged back, wrapped in a beige velour blanket, sipped spiced tea, and soaked in the warmth of the winter fire. Suddenly, I sensed the warmth and comfort of His presence and then His special request to me.

He whispered to my inner spirit, *I have a special request for you. Would you like to learn a new dance? I'll teach you step-by-step. I will always be right by your side. My Spirit will go before. I will take the lead. You will come to know Me as Jehovah-nissi — The Lord Is My Banner. I will be a banner before you, above, and behind you. I will reveal Myself to you in a completely new way. We'll experience a high adventure of faith. Will you accept?*

Inside me, thoughts whirled like a Midwest tornado. I answered with a conversational thud, "I don't think so!" Then I wrote tidily and politely in my prayer journal, "Uh, no thanks. I'll sit this one out." I continued with all the reasons why I shouldn't attempt anything outside of my faith comfort zone. The reasons made perfect sense:

- The timing was not right.
- I didn't have the qualifications.

131

- I didn't have the needed resources.
- And, it was too scary!

So again, I said, "I'll pass on this new dance, but I would love to waltz to my usual favorite song. I know all the steps, plus I am quite good at it now. OK, Lord?"

Then He brought to mind my friend Nicole. (I have changed her name to protect her identity.) Nicole believed she had received a special request from Jehovah-nissi — the Lord Is My Banner — to travel and live overseas as His ambassador. She accepted the special request even though it was far outside her comfort zone. Let me start at the beginning of Nicole's story.

UNEXPECTED SURGERY

I first met Nicole more than 15 years ago. She was a girl of elementary age, but she volunteered in the children's programs to help with the younger children. She loved kids and they loved her. Nicole's personality was sweet, but determined. She laughed easily, but asked thought-provoking questions too. When she was around 12 years old, the debilitating headaches began. The pain was so intense it caused her to curl into a fetal position to seek relief from any light that stabbed at her head. The headaches increased in intensity and frequency until the doctors finally discovered the root cause — a brain tumor.

My young, gentle friend was rushed to a children's hospital in San Francisco where she had surgery to remove the tumor. She was always petite, but the ravages of surgery and recovery shriveled her body into a tiny birdlike caricature. Her whittled body battled in league with painkillers and antibiotics that coursed through the IV for the next few weeks.

Thankfully, the surgery was successful in removing the tumor. And the biopsy proved the invading tissue was benign. Her family and our church rejoiced in the news.

However, the battle had just begun for Nicole; she was going to need months of rehabilitation. Nicole found herself in the physical condition of an infant — unable to care for herself. She lay in the hospital bed, dependent on someone else for her basic needs. She needed help feeding herself. She struggled to toddle around on her two spindly legs. Her life reversed from an active preadolescent to a dependent toddlerlike child — from skipping through hallways to leaning against her father's muscular arms.

Although our church prayed in earnest, it was hard to imagine Nicole ever being able to teach younger children to clap their hands and dance for Jesus again. Month after month passed. Progress was slow, but inch-by-inch, step-by-step, Nicole metamorphosed from a pale invalid to a teen who sparkled with physical health.

I became a small group leader for Nicole about three years after her surgery. Physically, she was fully recovered, but emotionally, she seesawed between her customary strong will and her postoperation fears. She would be dogmatic on some issues, but timid and fearful in other areas. She watched the other girls with reticence. I knew Nicole didn't always feel like she fit in. The other girls were anxious to drive, to date, and to depend on no one. They held one goal — to grow up. Nicole's personality proved to be different, in part, because of how God wired her and, in part, because of the tumor experience.

As a group, we chatted about what the future held for each girl. Marriage? Career? College? Adventure? I remember Nicole's look of perplexity. She enjoyed her today and didn't feel compelled to hurry life along. An overall quiet contentment for the present hovered over her. No one quite understood how Nicole, in the prime of young adulthood, could be so satisfied and not wish for the next steps toward adulthood.

Her satisfaction with life could be traced back to her tumor experience. Nicole understood better than we did how fragile life could be. She enjoyed the trivialities of life. God had taken her through a tough journey, and she was content being healthy. She required nothing more to spice up her life.

However, God had a plan for Nicole that not one of us would have imagined as we sat cross-legged on the carpet trying to predict our futures. In Nicole's future there floated a special request given to her by God.

SPECIAL REQUEST

God has a knack for asking us to do things that bring us way out of our comfort zone and make us depend on Him. Remember our friend Moses, who didn't feel he could lead the Hebrew slaves out of the bondage of the Egyptian dynasty? Remember, Moses didn't like the "special request" either.

However, God proved faithful to Moses and the children of Israel even when they would have preferred to stay in the comfort of their desert tents. One of the most challenging tasks was a battle with the nation of Amalekites who came upon the Israelites and attacked them. It was a long strenuous battle. A young commander, Joshua, fought the battle and Moses stood on a hill with a staff lifted high toward God. Scripture describes the scene.

As long as Moses held up his hands, the Israelites were winning, but whenever he lowered his hands, the Amalekites were winning. When Moses' hands grew tired, they took a stone and put it under him and he sat on it. Aaron and Hur held his hands up — one on one side, one on the other — so that his hands remained steady till sunset. So Joshua overcame the Amalekite army with the sword (EXODUS 17:11–13).

Moses built an altar and named it The LORD is My Banner (Exodus 17:14–15 NASB).

I find it odd that Moses had to hold his arms up while Joshua fought. What would be the point of that? But God did have a point to make — to Joshua. God wanted Joshua to be aware that He would be a banner of victory over Joshua. Scripture continues: "Then the LORD said to Moses, 'Write this in a book as a memorial and recite it to Joshua, that I will utterly blot out the memory of Amalek from under heaven.' Moses built an altar and named it The LORD is My Banner" (Exodus 17:14–15 NASB).

THE BANNER OF GOD

In ancient times, a banner was carried at the front of the army to indicate the line of march or a rallying point. The banner was attached to a long pole with a shiny adornment that would gleam in the sun and would be a marker so that the troops would be encouraged and motivated to continue with the orders of their commander.

Sometimes when God makes a special request it will involve a battle of some type; many times it is a battle with our own self-will. It might not be a physical war, but we will be asked to fight a battle of emotional or spiritual warfare. However, He will be the Banner over us despite the type of combat we are called into. Author Herbert Stevenson explains it in *Titles of the Triune God*, "In celebration of this victory, and as a memorial of their deliverance, 'Moses built an altar and called the name of it *Jehovah-nissi*' — which means, 'the LORD is my banner.' . . . This name appears in Scripture in this one text alone; but the thought expressed in it occurs repeatedly, on the lips of the psalmists and prophets."

"Make sure that Joshua hears it. . . . The LORD is my Banner." Interesting. Why did Joshua need to hear it and why did he need to know "The LORD Is My Banner"? Because God was going to make a very special request of Joshua, and it was going to be big, difficult, and scary.

A DANCE, A NEW BATTLE

The Lord wanted Joshua to learn a new dance in a new place. The Lord commanded Joshua to lead the children of Israel after the death of Moses. *And* He wanted him to take possession of the Promised Land — the land that God had promised to the children of Israel. There was one big quandary: it was infested by an array of enemy nations.

I think Joshua would have rather gone fishing than fighting. He didn't relish the idea of the conquering and conquest. Why? Joshua was scared. God kept reassuring

Joshua that He would be a banner over him as he fought. He repeated to Joshua:

> *"As I was with Moses, so I will be with you; I will never leave you nor forsake you. Be strong and courageous, because you will lead these people to inherit the land I swore to their forefathers to give them. Be strong and very courageous. . . . Have I not commanded you? Be strong and courageous. Do not be terrified; do not be discouraged, for the* LORD *your God will be with you wherever you go"* (JOSHUA 1:5–6, 7, 9).

For the Lord to repeat His message of assurance so many times indicates that Joshua felt weak, discouraged, and terrified. He didn't want to step out of the comfort zone of life, just like my friend Nicole, and just like me.

We are always afraid of failure. We ask ourselves, *What if I don't succeed at this new dance?* Of course, if we are obedient, then we are successful in the eyes of God. If we say *yes* to the invitation, then we have completed our element of the dance. It doesn't matter if the steps aren't beautiful and elegant — God is pleased with our obedience. To Him we are a success.

Joshua was a success story. Joshua most likely recalled these words of the Lord: "Write this up as a reminder to Joshua, 'God Is My Banner.'" Joshua decided to step out of his comfort zone, step up his faith, and step into the Promised Land. What was the end result of Joshua's dance into unknown territory? He led the children of Israel into the Promised Land with a resounding defeat of any who opposed them. Joshua never looked back to the comfort zone of his old desert home.

LAST STEP OF THE SPECIAL REQUEST

Eventually, Joshua grew old and it was time to pass the torch of leadership. Joshua reminisced about the events of his life and the Lord's involvement. He said, "Soon I will die, going the way of all the earth. Deep in your hearts you know that every promise of the LORD your God has come true. Not a single one has failed!" (Joshua 23:14 NLT). Jehovah-nissi certainly had been a banner to Joshua. God had gone with Joshua his entire life — He had never left him. Joshua closed his commencement speech with the familiar challenge, "But if serving the LORD seems undesirable to you, then choose for yourselves this day whom you will serve. . . . But as for me and my household, we will serve the LORD" (Joshua 24:15).

"But as for me and my household, we will serve the LORD" (Joshua 24:15).

DANCING ACROSS THE SEAS

Let me return to Nicole and the special request she sensed God making to her. In her early 20s, Nicole was staying busy going to college and working in a day-care center. (She still adored children.) Then she sensed a special request to dance with God to a new song in a foreign country. She believed God would have her to go to Thailand and teach children.

Nicole did not even hesitate. As I write, she is currently teaching in Thailand, learning a new language, a new culture, and a new dance of God. He was her banner in surgery, and He is her banner in Thailand. Like Joshua, she chooses to serve the Lord no matter where He asks her to go.

WILL YOU DANCE?

Susanne, will you dance a new dance? Will you serve as the church's women's ministries director?

I wiggled deeper into the chair and my cuddly blanket and resisted the Holy Spirit's invitation. However, images of Nicole and thoughts of her bravery, her self-sacrifice, and her adventure popped like kernels of popcorn before me.

Do I serve the Lord God? I asked myself. "Yes!" And I recognized my service couldn't be on my terms, but only on God's.

I picked up the phone and called my pastor. "Hey, Pastor Shane, if you can use my help, I would like to help the new church plant. I will volunteer as the women's ministry director."

"Perfect! I am so happy to hear that," responded my pastor.

"You know, Pastor Shane, God asks us to do things we would never dream of, doesn't He?"

"Like starting a church plant?"

"No, like me being a women's ministry director," I said.

"Well, He is the Lord and our guiding shepherd," Pastor Shane replied. "Welcome to ministry. And be thankful it isn't the Kiddie Kingdom!"

"Oh, I am!" I said with a laugh.

Dance Lesson

Read Song of Songs 2:4.

What type of banner is over us?

Read Ephesians 3:18.

What was the gist of the Apostle Paul's prayer for the Ephesians?

Read Romans 8:37.

List the things that cannot separate us from Christ's banner of love. What can separate us?

Read Isaiah 11:10.

Describe the banner found in this verse.

Read 2 Corinthians 2:14, and then compare it to Isaiah 11:10. What do you find that is similar?

What type of special request is God asking of you?

Will you say yes? Why or why not?

Advanced Dance Lesson

Read Joshua 2.

How is Rahab described?

Where did she live? What was her "comfort zone"?

What did Rahab do for the two Israelite spies?

Do you think she was afraid? Why or why not?

Read Joshua 6.

Describe what happened to the town of Jericho.

What did Joshua command in verses 22–23?

Read the genealogy of Jesus Christ in Matthew 1:1–6.

Whose name is mentioned in verse 8?

Describe your thoughts on Rahab being an ancestor to Jesus, our Jehovah-nissi.

Special Request Journal Page

Jot down your thoughts about Jehovah-nissi and any special request that He is asking you to dance.

~~~~~~
~~~~~~
~~~~~~
~~~~~~
~~~~~~
~~~~~~
~~~~~~
~~~~~~
~~~~~~
~~~~~~
~~~~~~
~~~~~~
~~~~~~
~~~~~~
~~~~~~
~~~~~~
~~~~~~
~~~~~~
~~~~~~
~~~~~~
~~~~~~

Hebrew Name: JEHOVAH-NISSI

Definition: THE LORD IS MY BANNER

Modern name: THE LORD IS MY BANNER

Party Banners

Party banners are an inexpensive way to decorate for any party or event. At most party stores, you can purchase ready-to-hang banners with preselected themes. Or you may create and order customized banners for an additional cost. Different types of banners are available: durable, vinyl banners for outdoor use or affordable, paper banners for short-term temporary use. Banners are the most economical way to create a theme and mood for the event.

Blisters AND *Bunions*

he bubbling water steamed my feet as I jumped back out of the shoes. I couldn't believe that I was that stupid. I had poured the boiling water into the shoes in an attempt to stretch the shoes that were too small for me. The adorable red flats had been handed down from a friend who had tired of them. They were *only* a half size too small. I figured I could stretch them out to fit. Another girlfriend told me to pour boiling water into the shoes, then to allow the wet leather to dry around my feet. One problem — I was so excited about the shoes, I forgot to allow the water to cool before sliding my feet into the shoes. Duh!

This episode taught me not to try to wear shoes that were never intended for my feet. But this precept doesn't just apply to shoes and feet; it applies to life's problems and God's grace.

BLISTERS ON THE SOUL

My thoughts rattled around like ice cubes clunking down into an ice bin. Writer's block locked my fingers against the keyboard. A melancholy mood prevented me from pursuing my own dance in intimacy with God. The soles of my spirit sported blisters and bunions. So how could I write about dancing with Him?

I was struggling with the ancient question, "Why do bad things happen to good people?" Well, not exactly all good people, but the people *I* love and care about—those people who intersect with me on a personal level. So, when two of my dearest friends struggled through separate heartbreaks within a six-month period, I began to feel spiritually lame. My question about *why* caused me to stumble instead of dance.

First, I need to explain how I tend to respond to life in general. Research studies reveal four personality types. These studies use various titles to classify the four types; however, regardless of the terms, they all agree to the basic components of the four personalities of human nature. I am going to use the expressions that I am most familiar with to help explain different character traits. Here are the four personality types:

◆ Sanguine: Extrovert, talker, optimistic
  • Bible personality: Apostle Peter
  • Music: Jazz
  • Dance: The jive
◆ Melancholy: Introvert, thinker, pessimist
  • Bible personality: Prophet Elijah
  • Music: The blues
  • Dance: Slow dance
◆ Choleric: Extrovert, doer, optimist
  • Bible personality: Moses
  • Music: Rock and roll
  • Dance: The hustle
◆ Phlegmatic: Introvert, watcher, pessimist
  • Bible personality: Doubting Thomas
  • Music: Country and western
  • Dance: Line dance

God created all of us. The Bible states, "Oh yes, you shaped me first inside, then out; you formed me in my mother's womb" (Psalm 139:13 *The Message*). Although we may be wired predominantly with one personality type, the Father wants us to become more like His Son, Jesus Christ, as stated in Romans 8:29 (*The Message*): "God knew what he was doing from the very beginning. He decided from the outset to shape the lives of those who love him along the same lines as the life of his Son. The Son stands first in the line of humanity he restored. We see the original and intended shape of our lives there in him." Jesus was the perfectly equal blend of all four personalities.

Usually, specific personality types are drawn to certain activities. Many artists, musicians, and writers fall into the category of the melancholy personality. You guessed it; I am, by nature, a melancholy. Over the years, God has sandpapered my melancholy raw and then healed me with His Holy Spirit. Throughout my years as a Christ-follower, my personality has been transformed — for the most part.

However, occasionally circumstances still rub me the wrong way. I develop a pessimistic blister in my attitudes. My relationship with God limps to the sideline, where I sit and mope about the unfairness and the injustice in the world.

As I discovered with my steamed tootsies, tender feet result in misery for the whole body. Most women *like* shoes, but I *adore* them. And, unfortunately, I do not always choose comfy shoes. I tend to pick footwear that looks fabulous but tortures the feet. My closet holds strappy summer sandals that rub my unwary skin into water-filled pockets of flesh throughout those warm summer months. My shoe rack exhibits high heels that pinch my toes into red nodular bumps across the knuckles of my toes. I try to prevent the likelihood of blisters by shaking white talcum powder liberally across my feet and into my "cute" shoes for the day. Or, my ten little piggies sport Dr. Scholl's toe pads for extra protection from those red, four-inch platform wedges. However, these precautionary tactics usually do nothing to thwart painful blisters.

A few months ago, I developed blisters on the soles of my feet *and* on the soul of my personality. The beaded discount sandals caused the pain in my feet, but the pain in my soul came from the devastating news that a close friend and co-worker in ministry had been diagnosed with Stage 4 lung cancer. Her prognosis was grim.

Three years earlier, I had watched my mother-in-law suffer horribly with the results of lung cancer. She fought the battle aggressively with chemotherapy, radiation, and surgery. She suffered through two years of intense depression and pain, finally ending in death. My mother-in-law had smoked for 50 years, but my friend had never smoked a cigarette in her life. My soul experienced a rub of unfairness and a poke of injustice.

THE HEALER

However, I continued to hobble along in my relationship with God. I didn't dance well, but I tried to shuffle along to keep in step with Him. A shadow fell across my heart. I wanted to ask why, but knew there would be no answer. I believed that *Jehovah-rapha*, the Lord who heals, could restore complete health to my cancer-stricken friend. In Exodus 15, God revealed His power to heal. The story goes like this.

The children of Israel had plodded through the Desert of Shur without any drinking water. They were tired, hot, and thirsty. Then to their delight, they stumbled onto water, but quickly discovered it was bitter and undrinkable. They were hot, tired, thirsty, and angry. They grumbled to Moses, "What are we supposed to drink?"

Without skipping a beat, the choleric Moses prayed to the Lord. Then he found an ordinary piece of splintery sun-bleached wood and tossed it into the water. Voilà — fresh sweet water provided for the grumpy crowd.

Then, the Lord decreed to the children of Israel that if they would listen carefully to His voice and do what was right, they would know Him as Jehovah-rapha. He said, "For I am the LORD, who heals you" (Exodus 15:26).

"For I am the LORD, who heals you" (Exodus 15:26).

In addition, throughout the New Testament we see Jesus healing multitudes of people: Jews, Gentiles, the righteous, and the deplorable. Jesus the healer — Jehovah-rapha. My favorite story of Jesus, our healer, is found in Mark 2. Four friends carried a disabled man to Jesus. But when they came to the house where Jesus sat, they found the crowd of people prohibited them from going further. The friends put their heads together and came up with a solution. They decided to haul the man up to the roof and lower him onto the floor before Jesus. Certainly not an easy task even for four strong men, but they cared enough to carry their disabled friend into the presence of the Lord. And yes, Jehovah-rapha healed the man and forgave his sins — a complete healing — thanks to the tenacity of four friends.

Now in my case, I felt sorrow for my friend and for myself. "Why? Why should my friend develop cancer?" I floated prayers heavenward, but melancholic thoughts stifled my faith.

A SPIRITUAL BUNION

In November of 2007, the spiritual melancholy spun into numb disbelief at another friend's tragedy. I progressed from mere blisters on my soul to a faith distortion. My trust in God twisted into six months of holding Him at arm's length. He was still my partner, but I kept Him at a distance. I didn't want to dance. God respected my desire — silence — no music. Eventually, I developed a spiritual bunion.

First, let me describe how a physical bunion occurs. It's an abnormal, bony bump that forms on the joint at the base of the big toe. The big toe joint becomes enlarged and painful. A bunion puts pressure on the surrounding bones and ligaments of the foot and leads to pain-filled movement of the foot. Bunions can occur for a number of reasons such as an inherited foot defect or an injury. However, the most common cause is women who cram their feet into shoes that are not the right fit. And not unexpectedly, dancers are especially susceptible to bunions because of the strain of the dance and ill-fitting dance shoes.

I danced with Jesus and I developed a relationship bunion. Here's what happened.

My girlfriend called me in tears, agony, and shock. Her 18-year-old son's body had been found three blocks from home. He was the victim of a random robbery and shooting. It made no sense. He had graduated from high school and had signed up to go into military service.

To make the tragedy even more painfully senseless, two years prior, this same mom had buried a 14-year-old son after he lost a battle with brain cancer. I could not imagine how she could cope with the double tragedy.

I sprang at God with indignation. "How could this happen? Where were You when David was walking on the sidewalk just a couple of blocks from home? It's not fair." Silence — no answer — no music — silence.

In December, I received the contract to write this book. My heart felt numb. I asked myself, *Should I sign the contract? Can I write a book about dancing in intimacy with God, the God who sees me, my Lord, the Lord who heals?* I felt so distant from Him. However, I signed the contract. I figured by January my relationship with God would be back on the spiritual dance floor and I would delight in writing the book.

However, January came and went. Writer's block prevented my thoughts from flowing into words for the book. In March, I felt concern. By May, I felt defeated and depressed. I asked my prayer and accountability group to pray for me. I told them I couldn't get past my friend's cancer diagnosis and my other beloved friend's loss of her children. I asked my friends to become a prayer shield for me.

Then, like the friends of the disabled man in the Book of Mark, my friends gathered in prayer and lifted my blistered faith to Jehovah-rapha. Unexpectedly, two different girlfriends recommended I reread *Why? Trusting God When You Don't Understand* by Anne Graham Lotz. I had read this book that dealt with faith, God, and the terrorist attack of September 11, 2001, but I decided it was time to reread it with a different lens. Lotz writes:

> *So often our primary ambition is to escape pain*
> *or feel good or be delivered from a problem when*

instead we need to keep our focus on the big picture of what God is doing in our life and the lives of others through pain or problems.... This trust in God to accomplish His primary purpose is eloquently expressed by the widow of Todd Beamer.... September 11, 2001, was the date of Todd Beamer's entrance into heaven. Lisa Beamer gave us a snapshot of her faith that is being developed through suffering when she told an interviewer, "God says, 'I knew on September 10, and I could have stopped it, but I have a plan for greater good than you can ever imagine.' I don't know God's plan, and, honestly, right now I don't like it very much. But I trust that He is true to His promise in Romans 8:28."

Yes, I knew Romans 8:28: "And we know that in all things God works for the good of those who love him, who have been called according to his purpose." I had heard this verse quoted tritely (and often by myself), but how does this "truth" apply to the pending death of my friend with cancer or to my girlfriend who lost two children in separate tragedies?

These questions on God's goodness clattered around in my mind like tin cans behind a speeding car. However, my friends — my faith-filled personal posse — kept handing me up before the throne room of God in prayer and in personal encouragement.

Next on the list of my own spiritual healing, a friend handed me the video *Life's Greater Purpose*, the story of Nick Vujicic. Nick, born without any arms or legs, is an international speaker who motivates people to believe in God's complete goodness, perfect love, and total faithfulness in their lives. I watched the video with amazement. Then Nick Vujicic spoke words that blew the clouds of melancholy away. In essence, the message was, "Many of you think that you could not, nor want to live, with my problems. But, truth be told, I would not trade mine for yours. See — God has given me the grace to bear mine; he hasn't given me the strength to bear yours."

Ah, relief! This truth was a healing balm on my blisters and bunions. I realized that I had taken on my friends' heartaches. Yes, I was supposed to pray for them. I should help with their needs, but I could not wrestle with God over what I deemed a fate "too harsh to bear." Now here's the funny part. In reality, both of my friends were dancing with God — it was I who had developed the wrong attitude. His grace was sufficient for them (2 Corinthians 12:9), but His grace was for them; it did not overflow to me if I chose to let their incalculable losses suppress my own faith.

HINDS' FEET

I had wedged my spiritual faith into someone else's troubles. The result? I developed blisters and bunions on my feet of faith because I had on the wrong dancing shoes. Ephesians 6:15 (NLT) advises, "For shoes, put on the peace that comes from the Good News, so that you will be fully prepared." For some reason I had always assumed that we put on our gospel shoes to go out and tell the world about Jesus. But a closer look at the definition from the original Greek word for peace, *eirēnē*, doesn't support my assumption to go witness; its true definition involves peace, calmness, and wholeness. God's shoes of peace provide a tranquil mind and an untroubled spirit. In other words, if you wear the corrective shoes of peace, you won't get blisters and bunions.

Yet, Jehovah-rapha knew the remedy. He allowed me to limp about for a time, so that when I finally sat down to write, I could tell my own story of His healing power over spiritual blisters and bunions that I caused by trying to fit my faith into someone else's life circumstance. Twice in Scripture it is written, "God is my strength and power: and he maketh my way perfect. He maketh my feet like hinds' feet: and setteth me upon my high places" (2 Samuel 22:33–34; Psalm 18:33 KJV).

In hindsight (no pun intended), I am thankful for the time to mull over God's goodness in life. While I slumped into a melancholy mood for months, I learned a valuable dance lesson — when horrific tragedies happen in life, it doesn't mean that God is out to get us, but it does mean that for the people who travel through them, the Lord who heals will provide the grace for them to dance. For us who are bystanders and friends, such as I was, we need to learn to wear the proper faith footwear, soles of peace, designed for our souls only. Our souls can overflow with peace — the peace from Jehovah-shalom.

He maketh my feet like hinds' feet, and setteth me upon my high places (Psalm 18:33 KJV).

Dance Lesson

Read Luke 5:1–26.

What types of "mats" do some of your friends lie on?

What keeps you from bringing your friends to Jesus? Busyness, embarrassment, etc.?

Do you have a mat of faithlessness that you lie upon?

Describe the friends in your life who are willing to carry you to Jesus.

Would you rather carry someone to Jesus or do you prefer your friends to carry you? Why?

Advanced Dance Lesson

Read John 5:1–8.

How long had the man been an invalid?

What question did Jesus ask the man in verse 6?

In your opinion, why do you think Jesus asked this question?

What did the man have to do to obtain his healing? (v. 8).

By completing the command of Jesus, how did the man answer the question in verse 6?

Do we sometimes have a part in our healing, whether physical, emotional, or spiritual? Explain.

Blisters and Bunions Journal Page

Jot down your thoughts about Jehovah-rapha — the Lord who heals — who has healed you.

~~~~~~

161

Hebrew name: JEHOVAH-RAPHA

Definition: THE LORD WHO HEALS

Modern translations: THE LORD WHO HEALS

Dancing Shoes

- Leather shoes are best because they breathe like skin and mold to your feet.
- Soles should be strong and flexible with a good gripping surface.
- Insoles should be cushioned to absorb the jolts of dancing.
- Good arch supports help distribute weight over a wider area of the feet.
- High heels look stylish and are fun but are not recommended for dancing.

Jitterbug

I stood in the aisle of the store considering the purchase of a new computer case. I held it. I unzipped the pockets. I sniffed the new leather. I opened the bag wide to inspect its depth. Unfortunately, I disturbed a large, ink-black cricket. It leapt onto my hand and twitched. It hopped and then perched itself on my arm. The antennae wiggled as if to say, "Hey, lady, you're disturbing my sleep."

Arghhh!!!!!

I screamed! I jerked! I jitterbugged. I danced as if I were on hot coals. I threw the bag.

The store clerk almost died of fright (not from the cricket, but from my frantic antics). She apologized repeatedly. Although she, too, was jittery about insects, she gallantly swept it out the door. Again, she apologized profusely.

My pounding heart slowed to a regular beat. I apologized to the clerk for my overreaction to the critter. We stood looking at each other with embarrassment. Finally, I broke the awkward silence. "Uh, I'll take the computer case," I said.

She responded with, "Well, I am giving you a 25 percent discount for this unfortunate incident."

A nightmare come true—but a bargain. I am still trying to figure out if it was worth it. Because my greatest phobia is anything that crawls with six or eight legs, just the thought of insects and spiders causes an anxiety attack. My nightmares consist of bugs scampering across my sheets and onto my skin. I awake brushing "things" off me. My husband shakes me to reality, "Susanne! There are no bugs."

FIREFLY FEARS

Fear flickers in our minds like a firefly on a dark night. It pops out of nowhere. Fear flashes a warning to our nervous systems with a rush of adrenaline-sponsored thoughts of fight or flight. Sometimes there is a valid reason. At other times, the irrational emotion erupts like a fire-breathing dragon—out of our imaginations.

The emotion of fear reminds me of the jitterbug. The jitterbug is a fast-paced dance, often without any type of recognizable steps. It is what is considered a spot dance where a couple takes over a small area of the dance floor and does their "own thing" without any forethought to the steps. They dance erratically, sometimes to the music, sometimes not. The dancers move with wild abandonment—oblivious to structured dance protocol.

Doesn't the jitterbug sound like fear? For me, fear stakes out territory in my thoughts. Trepidation steps out, then takes command, and pushes the uncontrolled worry into my thoughts. I lose my peace of mind.

And the peace of God, which transcends all understanding, will guard your hearts and your minds in Christ Jesus (Philippians 4:7).

164

Thankfully, God knows and understands our jittery fears. He comes to us as Jehovah-shalom — the Lord Is Peace. He is our peace. He wants us to allow Him to take over the dance floor of our thoughts. He wants to immerse us in His peace. Scripture says, "And the peace of God, which transcends all understanding, will guard your hearts and your minds in Christ Jesus" (Philippians 4:7).

THE LORD IS PEACE

Jehovah-shalom is the peace that allows us to maintain our sanity. He keeps our thoughts from racing higgledy-piggledy. When we allow His peace to reign over our fears, we can learn to ignore them or overcome them. We can stake out those places in our minds and allow God to flow His peace into those areas.

The first time we see God as Jehovah-shalom is in the Book of Judges. We see a scared young man hiding in a winepress to thresh his grain. Israel had been invaded by an enemy, the Midianites, who had kept them subjugated and impoverished. So, instead of threshing the grain out in the open, Gideon hides. But he cannot hide from God.

Gideon is threshing wheat when He hears the Lord say to him, "The LORD is with you, mighty warrior." God then commissions Gideon to free the Israelites from the dominion of the marauding Midianites.

Fear combusts into Gideon's thoughts. He stammers back with a first line of fear-filled defense, "But Lord." Here is Gideon's argument: "But LORD . . . how can I save Israel? My clan is the weakest in Manasseh, and I am the least in my family" (Judges 6:15). Have you ever felt that way? I know I certainly have. My fear cripples me into thinking I can do nothing—because I believe I am nothing.

However, God isn't impressed with our whining about being puny. He douses the flames of fear with the extinguishing guarantee of His presence. The Lord answers, "I will be with you, and you will strike down all the Midianites together" (Judges 6:16). The story continues with Gideon battling to overcome his fears and culminates with him discovering the peace of God.

> *When Gideon realized that it was the angel of the LORD, he cried out, "Sovereign LORD, I have seen the angel of the LORD face to face!"*
>
> *"It is all right," the LORD replied. "Do not be afraid. You will not die." And Gideon built an altar to the LORD there and named it "The LORD Is Peace"* (JUDGES 6:22–24 NLT).

The word *shalom* translates from the Hebrew as "peace." The definition expresses the deepest desire and need of a person's heart. It communicates complete satisfaction and contentment in life. Jehovah-shalom, the Lord is peace—our peace, our contentment, our satisfaction, and our well-being. When we jitterbug around in our fear-filled lives, He says, "Be still, and know that I am God" (Psalm 46:10). The

And Gideon built an altar to the LORD there and named it "The LORD Is Peace" (Judges 6:22–24 NLT).

Lord says, "Be still," to us. And even those words scare us!

For example, we read about this type of fearful response in the story of Jesus and His disciples crossing the stormy Sea of Galilee. Jesus, worn out from a long day of ministry, fell asleep, even though a storm was raging about their boat. The disciples, in a panic and fearful of drowning, woke Him. Here's what Jesus, our peace, did.

> *And he arose, and rebuked the wind, and said unto the sea, Peace, be still. And the wind ceased, and there was a great calm.*
>
> *And he said unto them, Why are ye so fearful? how is it that ye have no faith?*
>
> *And they feared exceedingly, and said one to another, What manner of man is this, that even the wind and the sea obey him?* (MARK 4:39–41 KJV).

After Jesus calmed the stormy weather, the disciples "feared exceedingly" about the nature of Jesus. I consider this a humorous ending to the story, but I know there are times in my own life when the power of God frightens me too.

TAKE AN INTERMISSION FROM STRESS

In addition, God's peace extends not only to our fears and doubts, but also to our crazy, stress-filled life. We jitterbug ourselves throughout the day's busyness. The term *jitterbug* came about because of a new approach to swing dancing. The swing dancers began to dance with a loss of traditional style. This new dance style of abandonment became known as jitterbugging. The dancers would jump around uncontrollably, making up a frenzy of dance steps as they went along. Have you ever felt that way? I have.

HERDING CHIPMUNKS

My sister-in-law and I recently took some toddlers to the park. It was like herding chipmunks. My grandson and my three nephews scampered in every direction. A play day outside seemed like a good idea. But the children, all under the age of five, had about an 18-second attention span. They wouldn't play in the same area. No one wanted to sit on the blanket for a picnic lunch. One boy slid headfirst down the slide. Another little guy rolled down a hill through a pile of doggie poo.

Finally, we decided to call it a day and take the little guys home. As we attempted to corral them on the picnic blanket, we neglected to count noses. As we scrambled to collect our belongings, we heard a commotion to the left of us. We turned only to realize ten or so adults were trying to rescue one of our boys teetering at the top of the very high monkey bars. He was crying, "Mama, Mama." We rushed over to the crisis and clambered up the bars to claim our three-year-old. Disaster averted. But the adults walked away shaking their heads at us as if to say, "Bad Mom; bad, bad Aunty; bad, bad, bad Grandma."

We were frazzled by the time we finally had them loaded up in their car seats with toys packed away. It was a chaotic day, leaving me jangled on the inside and craving a special treat—a coffee latte.

Now this was a poor choice. My high-strung self hardly needed anything more to stimulate me. But . . . I ordered the largest latte with an extra shot of espresso. Then I was wired high. The physiological effect of coffee on the human body is that it increases the blood circulation. It causes nervousness, and it can speed up a person's thoughts. My mind raced, and I felt like I could have jumped out of my skin. Coffee was the last thing I needed that day. What I needed was Jehovah-shalom to provide me His peace, not a peace from fear, but from stress. I should have turned to Him instead of the coffee shop. Here is what I would have found had I picked up my Bible.

- "Peace I leave with you; my peace I give you. I do not give to you as the world gives. Do not let your hearts be troubled and do not be afraid" (John 14:27).
- "May the God of hope fill you with all joy and peace as you trust in him" (Romans 15:13).
- "For God is not a God of disorder but of peace" (1 Corinthians 14:33).
- "For Christ himself is our way of peace" (Ephesians 2:14 TLB).

God's peace is not only a release from fear, but also a remedy for stress. He understands that often we spin out of control on the dance floor of life. Jehovah-shalom calls to our raging lives, "Peace, be still." Jesus said, "Come to me all you who are weary and burdened, and I will give you rest" (Matthew 11:28). The day I herded the chipmunk toddlers, I should have headed straight home for some quiet time, not a jolt of java.

INTERMISSION

What I needed was to be still — to take a pause — a *Selah*. This term is used throughout many of the Psalms. Although scholars are uncertain of its meaning, many believe it means to pause, to rest, or to consider. Selah may be an interlude or an intermission of the music — a time to stop, to take a breath, and to consider the lyrics of the song.

I think of the day Jesus wanted His disciples to take a Selah from ministry. The disciples had been busy with healing the sick, casting out demons, and preaching the good news of the kingdom of God. They returned exhausted, but on an emotional high. They wanted to tell Jesus about what they had experienced. But as crowds of people thronged about Jesus, they didn't even have a chance to eat. Then Jesus said, "Come with me by yourselves to a quiet place and get some rest" (Mark 6:31). He wanted them to take an intermission from ministry.

We are all called to service in the kingdom of God, but it should never turn into a marathon of frenzied activities. Our Lord of peace desires that we come away with Him and obtain a peace-filled perspective. He wants us to go into the stress-filled world and share His peace with love and joy. Who will listen to our words about God's peace if our own lives mirror a tilt-a-whirl at the summer carnival?

One of my favorite commercials currently is one in which a tired-looking woman is working on her laptop at night in the airport. She looks up at the camera and complains about various aspects of her busy life. Then she says, "I haven't had a day off since the third grade."

I recently witnessed this type of frenetic behavior in a fellow believer. I was speaking for a women's retreat held at a quaint, old Greek Orthodox retreat center. Arriving first, I tiptoed inside the silence of the building. The cold masonry stonework cooled the air as I stood wondering where I should go.

Then I heard a scurrying down a long hallway. A monk appeared, wearing a long royal blue robe with a golden sash tied around the waist. A golden pillbox hat perched on top of a bush of gray hair that extended down with sideburns ending in a whiskery white beard. He approached me wringing his hands. His blue eyes bulged with a wary alarm.

"Are you with the church group? he asked.

"I am the speaker, but I am early. Have the others arrived yet?" I responded.

"You're late! Come with me! I need to show you the regulations. I'm behind my schedule," he said.

I insisted that he wait until the retreat director came. He scowled at me and then hurried back down a dark hallway. That was only the beginning of our experience with the agitated man of faith. At mealtime, he would clang a large bell as an "invitation" to come eat. He would scold, "Hurry, hurry, the food is waiting."

In contrast, the cook was a petite, smiling woman with a crop of dark hair that bounced as she scooped our plates full. Her laugh echoed against the stone walls. This woman welcomed us with an acute joy.

Disaster struck the next morning at breakfast. The happy cook slipped on a wet tile and broke her right arm just below the elbow. The monk went into a frenzy, insisting that she stay until after lunch so she could cook and serve our group. We were aghast. We argued that she needed to go to the hospital and have her arm set in a cast. He stood in stoic denial of this fact. However, we wouldn't budge in our opinion either. Finally, he grudgingly allowed one of our women to take her for medical attention.

He repeated over and over to himself, "I don't know what to do. This is very irregular. What should I do?"

We attempted to calm him, but to no avail. At last, we left the dining area and continued with the retreat program.

To our chagrin, when we entered the hall for lunch, there stood the beaming cook with her arm in a cast, endeavoring to ladle out the food. The sour-faced man of faith would not meet our eyes. He stood on guard in the wooden door frame of the kitchen and watched morosely as we inquired how she felt.

We left the following morning to the warm good-byes of the winsome woman who still demonstrated tranquillity. The man still scurried, hurried, and worried. He escorted us out the door and then slammed it firmly. We heard him mutter, "Everything is so out of order. Very irregular!"

This schedule-tormented man desperately needed Jehovah-shalom. He required the spiritual tranquilizer of peace that only God can supply. No matter how trying and stressful our lives may become, God holds the peace that will surpass our understanding in its ability to soothe us.

I hope the next time I am fearful, or worried, or emotionally uptight, I remember this manic monk. I want the memory of him to be a reminder not to jitterbug through life, but to allow Jehovah-shalom to bring His peace to me. And I pray this individual, this fellow believer, will find serenity for his spirit, peace for his purpose, and rest in his regimented routine. I pray the Shepherd will come and lead him beside still waters and make him lie down in green pastures of peace.

Dance Lesson

Read Judges 6:23–40.

What did the Lord declare to Gideon in verse 23?

How did Gideon respond to the Lord?

What emotion did Gideon experience in verse 27?

Describe the requests of Gideon and the responses of the Lord.

Read Judges 8:28.

What was the outcome of Gideon's experience?

How do you relate to Gideon?

How can you experience God's peace in your life?

Advanced Dance Lesson

Read the Scriptures below.

How can you apply each one to your life?

Therefore, since we have been justified through faith, we have peace with God through our Lord Jesus Christ (Romans 5:1).

I will lie down and sleep in peace, for you alone, O LORD, make me dwell in safety (Psalm 4:8).

You will keep in perfect peace him whose mind is steadfast, because he trusts in you (Isaiah 26:3).

Those who love your law have great peace and do not stumble (Psalm 119:165 NLT).

The Lord *gives his people strength. The* Lord *blesses them with peace* (Psalm 29:11 NLT).

"I am leaving you with a gift—peace of mind and heart. And the peace I give isn't like the peace the world gives. So don't be troubled or afraid" (John 14:27 NLT).

Jitterbug Journal Page

Jot down your thoughts about your fears, your stress, Jehovah-shalom, and His peace.

~~~~~~
~~~~~~
~~~~~~
~~~~~~
~~~~~~
~~~~~~
~~~~~~
~~~~~~
~~~~~~
~~~~~~
~~~~~~
~~~~~~
~~~~~~
~~~~~~
~~~~~~
~~~~~~
~~~~~~
~~~~~~
~~~~~~
~~~~~~
~~~~~~
~~~~~~

Hebrew: JEHOVAH-SHALOM

Definition: GOD IS PEACE

Modern translations: GOD IS PEACE

Intermission Coffee Bar

- Ceramic mugs or sturdy hot drink cups
- Fresh tea and hot coffee
- Sugar and artificial sweeteners
- Cold milk or cream
- A variety of flavored coffee syrups: vanilla, hazelnut, mocha

Chaperone Shepherd

I rushed from the sparkling spring sunshine into the smell of the antiseptic hospital. I remembered thinking, *Who would have thought I would be at a hospital today? Life turns on a dime.*

The phone had jangled at 7:00 A.M. It was my daughter-in-law. She was taking my son to the hospital. "He can't breathe. He says it feels like his throat is being torn out when he swallows."

"I'll meet you there," I said.

This began a long 24 hours. My son was admitted into the emergency room immediately. His uvula, the little piece of flesh that dangles in the back of the throat, was swollen to the size of a large apple. His throat looked as if it had been scraped with a rake. The doctors were not exactly sure what was wrong. They ran blood tests. Oxygen flowed from a slender tube into my son's nose to aid his breathing. An IV pushed antibiotics and steroids into his bloodstream.

My daughter-in-law and I took turns pacing the hallways pushing my nine-month-old grandson in the stroller. We asked questions to which there were no answers. Prayers shot spontaneously toward heaven. Our cell phones rang with calls from concerned friends and relatives. Our lives changed in a moment's time—from carefree to caregiving.

Eventually evening arrived, but my son was no better. I sent my daughter-in-law and grandson home to sleep. I told her I would stay with him at the hospital for the night. There were no rooms in the hospital available, so we were required to stay in the emergency room. We prayed for God's peace to enter into the room where chaos and worry had ruled.

STILL WATERS

I settled into a hard plastic chair by my son's bed. I picked up my Bible and thumbed through it. I read the Twenty-third Psalm.

> *The LORD is my shepherd, I shall not be in want.*
> *He makes me lie down in green pastures,*
> *He leads me beside quiet waters,*
> *he restores my soul.*
> *He guides me in paths of righteousness*
> *for his name's sake.*
> *Even though I walk*
> *through the valley of the shadow of death,*
> *I will fear no evil,*
> *for you are with me;*
> *your rod and your staff,*
> *they comfort me.*
> *You prepare a table before me*
> *in the presence of my enemies.*
> *You anoint my head with oil;*
> *my cup overflows.*
> *Surely goodness and love will follow me*
> *all the days of my life,*

*and I will dwell in the house of the L*ORD
  forever.

The familiarity of the psalm brought comfort to me. I thought about God as my shepherd, as my son's shepherd, and as the shepherd of everyone who scurried around the hospital that night. Even as I sat in the stiff-backed chair and listened to my son gasp for air, I was reassured God was in control. This certainty kept away the jitterbug of worry and brought me to a place of Selah, of peace, despite the circumstance. The Lord came as my shepherd to chaperone me through the dark night into an unknown dance.

*The L*ORD *is my shepherd, I shall not be in want. He makes me lie down in green pastures, he leads me beside quiet waters (Psalm 23:1).*

SLINGSHOT FAITH

The Twenty-third Psalm brought me confidence, especially when I considered the author, King David. David was a man familiar with turmoil, missteps, and loneliness when he penned Psalm 23. David knew stress, fear, and heartache. He had been a fugitive on the run, he had fought fierce battles, and he had opposed a terrorizing enemy named Goliath.

Yes, this was the man who killed Goliath with a slingshot while everyone else trembled in terror. David was a young man at the time he faced the Philistine giant in battle with only his slingshot and his faith in God. How did David dare to do it?

Because he trusted in the care of God more than the appearance of the circumstances. David phrased it this way: "You come against me with sword and spear and javelin, but I come against you in the name of the LORD Almighty, the God of the armies of Israel, whom you have defied. . . . All those gathered here will know that it is not by sword or spear that the LORD saves; for the battle is the LORD's, and he will give all of you into our hands" (1 Samuel 17:45, 47).

David was not only a warrior, but also a skilled musician and an articulate poet. David expressed his personal relationship with God as *Jehovah-rohi* — The Lord Is My Shepherd. He was the first to reveal the nature of God as a shepherd who cared deeply and protectively about His sheep.

An actual shepherd and author W. Phillip Keller put into plain words our relationship with God as our shepherd. He writes in *A Shepherd Looks at Psalm 23*:

> *Now the beautiful relationships given to us repeatedly in Scripture between God and man are those of a father to his children and a shepherd to his sheep. These concepts were first conceived in the mind of God our Father. They were made possible and practical through the work of Christ.*

David, the author of the poem, himself a shepherd and the son of a shepherd, later to be known as the "Shepherd King" of Israel, stated explicitly, "The Lord is my shepherd." To whom did he refer?

He referred to Jehovah, the Lord God of Israel.

His statement was confirmed by Jesus the Christ. When He was God incarnate amongst men, He declared emphatically, "I am the good shepherd."

David's caretaking of his father's flocks gave him the personal awareness of how a shepherd protects and cares for his sheep. He fed, guided, and protected the flocks. He had killed a lion and a bear to defend his flock. King David recognized God's heart as a shepherd, because David was a shepherd.

David understood sheep. He knew people. He realized that there was a similarity between the two — the greatest being that both people and sheep need a guiding caregiver. Sheep are defenseless against predators. They require a shepherd to take care of them. Kay Arthur explains their predicament:

> If sheep do not have the constant care of a shepherd, they will go the wrong way, unaware of the dangers at hand. They have been known to nibble themselves right off a mountainside! They will overgraze the land and run out of food unless the shepherd leads them to new pastures, and if they are not led to proper pastures, they will obliviously eat or drink things that are disastrous to them. Sheep easily fall prey to predators, and when they do, they are virtually defenseless. Sheep can also become cast down and, in that state, panic and die. And so, because sheep are sheep, they need shepherds to care for them.

LOST ON THE DANCE FLOOR

We are the sheep. Instead of looking to Jehovah-rohi for guidance, we stumble around on the dance floor of life looking for the purpose of life and seeking happiness. *The Message* describes us: "We're all like sheep who've wandered off and gotten lost. We've all done our own thing, gone our own way" (Isaiah 53:6).

We bleat our complaints to anyone who will listen. We rummage around in pleasures looking for fulfillment. We wander off looking for a better life, although God is waiting to guide us into green pastures. However, when we admit our needs and dependency, the Shepherd will guide us through any hardship life tosses at us. We will discover the truth and comfort of His staff even though we sit unexpectedly in a hospital emergency room; He will be with us through the shadow of death.

When we follow Jehovah-rohi, He will meet our needs. It will not matter if we face financial collapse, terrorists' plots, or natural disasters. We can state firmly, "I will fear no evil, for you are with me; your rod and your staff, they comfort me" (Psalm 23:4). We must allow Him to chaperone us into the dance of protector and protected.

CALM AMIDST CRISIS

I read Psalm 23 again. I prayed it. Then I witnessed His chaperoning in my son's hospital room. I watched countless episodes of Jehovah-rohi—the Shepherd—herd His children, His sheep, into a place of rest and comfort. Some of those people held no knowledge that God was at work. It was as if an invisible master musician stepped in to orchestrate peace and comfort over the pain and sickness that threatened to overtake the emergency room. I watched God work through human hands and hearts to help the men and women in distress.

It began with my son. He was miserable. He hadn't slept for more than 24 hours. For him to breathe, he was required to sit up. If he tried to lie down, his throat felt like it was closing. He sat with his head hung over a plastic hospital container. Drool slid from his mouth into the bowl. However, the caring nurses came in every few minutes to check on him. Each nurse was kind with a gentle sense of humor. When they strolled into the room, it seemed as if a fragrant breath of fresh air wafted in. I watched as they attempted to make my son as comfortable as possible. They were patient with him as they encouraged him to try to lie back in his bed. I witnessed through their human hands the hands of God at work. I thought of the verse, "I myself will tend my sheep and have them lie down, declares the Sovereign LORD" (Ezekiel 34:15).

THE WRONG DANCE FLOOR

A homeless man shared the room with only a sallow blue curtain hanging between him and my son. Around the curtain, I could see his long, dirty hair pulled up into a ponytail. A gloved technician lightly wrapped his filthy feet in elastic bandages in an attempt to protect the sanitary surroundings of the hospital. The stab wounds to his thigh were cleansed thoroughly as he held an incomprehensible conversation with the attendant.

"Where am I? Is this the Hilton hotel?" he asked.

"No, sir, you are in the emergency room," replied the technician.

"I want my coffee. Now! I want it hot with lots of cream and sugar," the patient demanded.

"Sir, we'll bring you coffee with your breakfast later this morning."

"Where am I? Am I on a cruise ship?

"No, sir, you're in the hospital," said the attendant.

"Where's my coffee?"

This type of conversation continued for hours, but not once did I see any of the hospital staff reflect irritation. It was as if a peace had descended into the room to comfort not only my son but also the vagrant and the harried hospital staff. I witnessed the truth of Isaiah 40:11: "He tends his flock like a shepherd: He gathers the lambs in his arms and carries them close to his heart." I watched the Good Shepherd in action that night through the hearts and hands of others.

My son recovered, although they never discovered exactly what had caused the debilitating episode. It was back to life as usual. The everyday blessings and hassles occurred, but now I viewed them through different eyes. I was dancing through life, but I knew I had the chaperoning Shepherd guiding me with His staff.

Shortly after this realization, my husband and I were driving in southern Utah on our way to Bryce Canyon National Park. Suddenly, we were halted atop the winding mountain road. A flock of sheep meandered across the highway. They sashayed their way across the road to munch on a few mouthfuls of grass. The shepherd tried to hurry them across the asphalt, but to no avail.

Although several cars were delayed on their way up to the park, no one seemed to mind. The people in the cars enjoyed watching the wooly procession — sheep and their shepherd making their way through life.

As we waited for the road to clear, I remembered the blessing in the hospital a few weeks earlier. My imagination took over and a few reflections floated through my mind — sheep thoughts.

SHEEP THOUGHTS

Sheep thought: *I belong to no one.*

The Shepherd says, "You are my flock, the sheep of my pasture. You are my people, and I am your God, says the Sovereign LORD" (Ezekiel 34:31 NLT).

Sheep thought: *I am lost.*

The Shepherd says, "For this is what the Sovereign LORD says: I myself will search for my sheep and look after them" (Ezekiel 34:11).

Sheep thought: *No one cares.*

The Shepherd says, "When Jesus landed and saw a large crowd, he had compassion on them, because they were like sheep without a shepherd" (Mark 6:34).

Sheep thought: *I am afraid.*

The Shepherd says, "I am the good shepherd. The good shepherd lays down his life for the sheep" (John 10:11).

Sheep thought: *This is my shepherd!*

The Shepherd says, "I am the good shepherd; I know my sheep and my sheep know me" (John 10:14).

Final sheep thought:

> GOD, *my shepherd!*
> > *I don't need a thing.*
> *You have bedded me down in lush meadows,*
> > *you find me quiet pools to drink from.*
> *True to your word,*
> > *you let me catch my breath*
> > *and send me in the right direction.*
> *Even when the way goes through*
> > *Death Valley,*
> *I'm not afraid*
> > *when you walk at my side.*
> *Your trusty shepherd's crook*
> > *makes me feel secure.*
> *You serve me a six-course dinner*
> > *right in front of my enemies.*
> *You revive my drooping head;*
> > *my cup brims with blessing.*
> *Your beauty and love chase after me*
> > *every day of my life.*
> *I'm back home in the house of GOD*
> > *for the rest of my life*
> > (PSALM 23:1–6 THE MESSAGE).

As we dance through life, we have a chaperone shepherd — Jehovah-rohi. He guides us to green pasture for rest. God protects us. Jesus cares for us in every need of life. He is our Good Shepherd.

I quoted W. Phillip Keller earlier and I want to remind us of his words. He points out the two primary relationships in

"I am the good shepherd; I know my sheep and my sheep know me" (John 10:14).

the Bible concerning God and His children: "Now the beautiful relationships given to us repeatedly in Scripture between God and man are those of a father to his children and a shepherd to his sheep."

Today we danced with the Good Shepherd, but next we will dance with our Father—a relationship beyond our "sheep thought" comprehension.

Our Daddy is waiting to embrace us in His everlasting arms.

Dance Lesson

Read John 10:1–18.

Compare and contrast it to Psalm 23.

How does Jesus fulfill the complete role of the Shepherd described in Psalm 23?

191

Below read the paraphrased Psalm 23. In the blanks, write your name and then rest in the knowledge He is *your* shepherd. Believe it!

The Lord is _____'s shepherd, _____ shall not be in want.

He makes _____ lie down in green pastures, he leads _____ beside quiet waters, he restores _____'s soul. He guides _____ in paths of righteousness for his name's sake.

Even though _____ walks through the valley of the shadow of death, _____ will fear no evil, for you are with _____ ; your rod and your staff, they comfort _____.

You prepare a table before _____ in the presence of _____'s enemies. You anoint _____'s head with oil; _____'s cup overflows.

Surely goodness and love will follow _____ all the days of _____'s life, and _____ will dwell in the house of the Lord forever.

Advanced Dance Lesson

Read the following verses and write what they teach you about Jehovah-rohi.

Hebrews 13:20–21:

1 Peter 2:25:

1 Peter 5:4:

Revelation 7:17:

193

Read Matthew 9:35–37 and answer the following questions.

How can we show compassion to others?

What opportunities do you have to serve in your community and care for the needs of others? (prisons, hospitals, women's shelters, etc.).

When we serve others with love and compassion, how do we reflect the qualities of our own Good Shepherd?

Chaperone Shepherd Journal Page

Jot down your thoughts concerning how the Good Shepherd watches over you.

~~~~~~
~~~~~~
~~~~~~
~~~~~~
~~~~~~
~~~~~~
~~~~~~
~~~~~~
~~~~~~
~~~~~~
~~~~~~
~~~~~~
~~~~~~
~~~~~~
~~~~~~
~~~~~~
~~~~~~
~~~~~~
~~~~~~
~~~~~~
~~~~~~

Hebrew name: Jehovah-rohi

Definition: The Lord Is My Shepherd

Modern name: Good Shepherd

A Care Station

To make sure your guests are comfortable, make a "green pasture" station.

Have a secure place where guests may leave their coats and bags.

Provide a basket with miscellaneous items such as:

- Breath mints
- Aspirin
- Tissues
- Feminine products
- Hand lotion

Embraced

BY THE *Father*

*H*er smile lit up the room when her daddy entered the room. Her rosebud lips spread into a wide beam of a smile. Her silky black hair leapt about her face as she bounced excitedly on the balls of her feet. She looked like Snow White after a large cup of espresso. The man started the music and began to walk toward her. He stopped and opened wide his muscular arms — the familiar invitation to dance. She raced to him and perched herself atop his feet. They began two-stepping to their special song, "My Personal Penguin." The princess was dancing with her Prince Charming — her daddy.

Bittersweet joy washed over me like a warm spring rain as I witnessed this scene between my son and granddaughter. Happiness for my granddaughter flowed into my heart, but there was also a tinge of sadness. I regretted never having experienced the same type of father-daughter relationship with my earthly dad.

My father resembled the character of Rhett Butler from *Gone with the Wind*. He was suave, handsome, and self-assured, but a rogue. I traveled through my childhood and adolescence wishing for a Rhett Butler type of man to whisk me off my feet. I desired a rogue to embrace me with a wild and untamed love.

Because of my "father image," I actually desired imperfect love from the people I loved the most. A flawed love would hurt, but it still appealed to my broken heart. I believed falsely that love could only be achieved through volatile sparks of emotion, fueled by the uncertainty of the love.

Of course, it was all a misguided representation of a girl's broken heart. My heart was a lace Valentine — the right shape, but with holes nicked out. Thankfully, my heavenly Father was able to fill those holes in my heart with a perfect love. The night I accepted His offer to dance the wallflower waltz, He began to reveal to me the character of a faultless Father. As the Father embraced me, my idea of errant love slid into oblivion. I learned the true meaning of love as I gained knowledge of God. He taught me His characteristics and personality through the diversity of His names, but my favorite will always be Father — *Abba* — my Daddy.

ABBA

In the New Testament, Jesus distinguished the name of Father for God. Jesus taught His disciples to use the Aramaic *abba*, a term of affection that approximates our English word *Daddy*, to address the heavenly Father. Jesus illustrated this when He taught the disciples how to pray.

> *"But when you pray, go away by yourself, shut the door behind you, and pray to your Father secretly. Then your Father, who knows all secrets, will reward you . . . your Father knows exactly what you need even before you ask him! Pray like this:*

Our Father in heaven,
  may your name be honored.
May your Kingdom come soon.
May your will be done here on earth,
  just as it is in heaven.
Give us our food for today,
and forgive us our sins,
  just as we have forgiven those who have sinned
  against us.
And don't let us yield to temptation,
  but deliver us from the evil one"
  (MATTHEW 6:6–13 NLT).

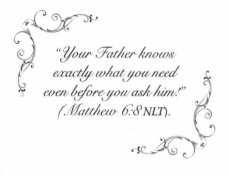

"Your Father knows exactly what you need even before you ask him!" (Matthew 6:8 NLT).

This lesson on prayer, asking our heavenly Father, includes all the basic needs. Jesus wanted His followers to know that God, the Father, would take care of His children better than an earthly dad ever could. He knew what they needed before they asked. He would provide for their physical, emotional, and spiritual needs. He was their daddy.

THE FATHER-DAUGHTER DANCE

This thought of a father providing for the daughter is demonstrated at weddings. The stoic dad walks the tearful, but joyous, bride down the aisle and releases her to the care of the bridegroom. At the wedding reception after the ceremony, the father and daughter dance together — alone on the dance floor.

My niece participated in this tradition at her reception recently. Her dad took her into his arms and they danced to "I Loved Her First." There was not a dry eye in the house. (It would have been a good day to have stock in tissues.) It was true he had loved her first — before the groom — but not before God.

This is true of our relationship with the Father. He loved us before the beginning of time, before we were born, and He will love us when we pass from this earth. Scripture tells us we have the ability to love others because God loved us first, "We love each other as a result of his loving us first" (1 John 4:19 NLT).

It's hard for us to fathom this type of loving relationship with God. But He is our Abba whether we believe it or not. He rejoices over us. Can you imagine placing your feet on His and allowing Him to guide you, delight in you, and sing over you just as my son does for my granddaughter? It's hard to imagine, but Zephaniah 3:17 says, "The LORD your God is with you, he is mighty to save. He will take great delight in you, he will quiet you with his love, he will rejoice over you with singing."

AND SO MUCH MORE

Our Abba is more than we can ever envision or understand. The *Holman Bible Dictionary* explains this mystery far better than I can.

> *God is unique in nature. No person, object, or idea*
> *can be adequately compared to God. Anything said*

about God must be based on His revelation of Himself to us. Anything said about God must be said in human terms, the only terms we have and understand. The reality of God is always much greater than human minds can understand or express. . . . God is Father. The love of God finds supreme expression as Father. God is known in Scripture as Father in three separate senses that must not be confused: (1) He is Father of Jesus Christ in a unique sense — by incarnation; (2) He is Father of believers — by adoption or redemption; (3) He is Father of all persons — by creation.

So, the heavenly Father is the father of Jesus Christ, the Son of God, by a mystery that we cannot fully comprehend. We are His children through adoption by the death and resurrection of Jesus if we receive Him as our Savior. And in a general sense, God is the Father of all creation. These are the distinctive quantifiers of God as Father. However, Scripture also gives us other traits of God's fatherhood to us.

- The everlasting Father (Isaiah 9:6)
- Father of compassion (2 Corinthians 1:3)
- Father of our spirits (Hebrews 12:9)
- Father of the heavenly lights (James 1:17)
- Father to the fatherless (Psalm 68:5)

Because of all these aspects of God's fatherhood, we can move into an even more intimate relationship with Him. He wants us to understand how to relate to Him as Daddy, as Abba. "And because you . . . have become his children, God has sent the Spirit of his Son into your hearts, and now you can call God your dear Father" (Galatians 4:6 NLT). He is our Abba, the everlasting compassionate Daddy. I once had the privilege of witnessing Abba's gentle love, a reassuring love in a friend's life and ministry.

> *And because you . . . have become his children, God has sent the Spirit of his Son into your hearts, and now you can call God your dear Father (Galatians 4:6 NLT).*

NOT AS EXPECTED

My friend grew up in a respected Christian home. Her earthly father served in full-time vocational ministry while her mother stayed home and raised the four children. They traveled across the United States in the summer as her father toured in ministry. My friend watched people cluster around him in praise and adoration. But no more than she did—she adored her daddy.

Life continued along this idyllic path. Love, faith, and stability set the foundation for the family—until she turned 16. At that time, her father came home and made an announcement. He was going to leave the family and marry another woman. My friend's heart shattered into pieces of insecurity, heartache, and spiritual doubt.

My friend struggled with qualms of God's love and faithfulness for years. God slowly mended her faith into one piece again. Eventually, she decided to trust Him again. She acknowledged His love for her—but she would never allow herself to be called into ministry. She deemed the subtle human frailty side of ministry destroyed her family. She could not trust herself not to fail as her daddy had failed.

FOR THE LOVE OF CHOCOLATE

But soon, she was called. She resisted, but finally attended the Proverbs Ministries She Speaks! conference. (This conference's purpose is to help women discern their ministry callings in areas such as writing, speaking, and leadership.) I had known my friend from a previous association, and she asked if she could be my roommate for the weekend. I assured her I would be delighted to have her for a roomie and the arrangements were made.

I arrived at the hotel first and went up to our room. As I unloaded my suitcase, I noticed the light flashing on the room phone. I picked it up to hear I had a special delivery package. *That's odd*, I thought, as I was not expecting anything. I tramped back down to the lobby registration desk, where they handed me a light, but quite large box.

Back in the room, I began to unwrap the package. To my surprise and delight, it was a large three-pound box of Godiva chocolates. There was not time to sample the treat before my first meeting, so I placed it on a table.

Later that night my friend and I finally met up in our room. She looked at me with wide eyes and said, "Susanne, you haven't opened those Godiva chocolates!"

I had forgotten all about the chocolate confection. "Oh, a friend from Nevada sent them to me as a surprise gift. Want one?" I responded.

"Oh, yes!" she said as she carefully untied the gold foil ribbon.

We stayed up late chatting, laughing, and gorging ourselves with the rich chocolates.

Suddenly she said wistfully, "Did I ever tell you that my dad used to take us kids out once a month for a 'date'? This quality time always ended with a trip to the Godiva chocolate store and the purchase of a candy of our choice. I still hold that tradition close to my heart — it reminds me of happier memories. In fact, I do it with my kids now."

Then I realized why the chocolates were a special delivery to us. Although my friend sent them, they weren't for me.

"These chocolates weren't for me," I said. "These chocolates were for you — from God. Only He would know how much Godiva chocolate meant to you."

With the light of this knowledge, she smiled with tears in her eyes. "I guess I should trust Him and His calling, huh?"

"Yeah, I think so," I said and handed her another chocolate. "Would you like to pack the bow and ribbon to take home? And are you saying yes to the Father?"

"Yes to both questions," she said with chocolate-smeared teeth.

My friend accepted the full embrace of the Father as found in Romans 8:15 (NLT): "You should not be like cowering, fearful slaves. You should behave instead like God's very own children, adopted into his family — calling him 'Father, dear Father.'"

[We call] him "Father, dear Father" (Romans 8:15 NLT).

THE FATHER'S LOVE LETTER TO YOU

Often when I speak at a retreat, I close with an extraordinary audio reading, "The Father's Love Letter." My heart is full of gratitude to the author, Barry Adams, and his ministry, the Father Heart Communications, for granting me permission to share this treasure with you.

The Father's Love Letter

My Child,

> *The Words you are about to experience are true.*
> *They will change your life if you let them.*
> *For they come from the very heart of God.*
> *He loves you.*
> *And He is the Father you have been looking for all of your life.*

This is His love letter to you.

> *You may not know me, but I know everything about you. Psalm 139:1*
> *I know when you sit down and when you rise up. Psalm 139:2*
> *I am familiar with all your ways. Psalm 139:3*
> *Even the very hairs on your head are numbered. Matthew 10:29–31*
> *For you were made in my image. Genesis 1:27*
> *In me you live and move and have your being. Acts 17:28*
> *For you are my offspring. Acts 17:28*
> *I knew you even before you were conceived. Jeremiah 1:4–5*
> *I chose you when I planned creation. Ephesians 1:11–12*
> *You were not a mistake, for all your days are written in my book. Psalm 139:15–16*

I determined the exact time of your birth and where you would live. Acts 17:26

You are fearfully and wonderfully made. Psalm 139:14

I knit you together in your mother's womb. Psalm 139:13

And brought you forth on the day you were born. Psalm 71:6

I have been misrepresented by those who don't know me. John 8:41–44

I am not distant and angry, but am the complete expression of love. 1 John 4:16

And it is my desire to lavish my love on you. 1 John 3:1

Simply because you are my child and I am your Father. 1 John 3:1

I offer you more than your earthly father ever could. Matthew 7:11

For I am the perfect father. Matthew 5:48

Every good gift that you receive comes from my hand. James 1:17

For I am your provider and I meet all your needs. Matthew 6:31–33

My plan for your future has always been filled with hope. Jeremiah 29:11

Because I love you with an everlasting love. Jeremiah 31:3

My thoughts toward you are as countless as the sand on the seashore. Psalm 139:17–18

And I rejoice over you with singing. Zephaniah 3:17

I will never stop doing good to you.
Jeremiah 32:40

For you are my treasured possession.
Exodus 19:5

I desire to establish you with all my heart and all my soul. Jeremiah 32:41

And I want to show you great and marvelous things. Jeremiah 33:3

If you seek me with all your heart, you will find me. Deuteronomy 4:29

Delight in me and I will give you the desires of your heart. Psalm 37:4

For it is I who gave you those desires.
Philippians 2:13

I am able to do more for you than you could possibly imagine. Ephesians 3:20

For I am your greatest encourager.
2 Thessalonians 2:16–17

I am also the Father who comforts you in all your troubles. 2 Corinthians 1:3–4

When you are brokenhearted, I am close to you. Psalm 34:18

As a shepherd carries a lamb, I have carried you close to my heart. Isaiah 40:11

One day I will wipe away every tear from your eyes. Revelation 21:3–4

And I'll take away all the pain you have suffered on this earth. Revelation 21:3–4

I am your Father, and I love you even as I love my son, Jesus. John 17:23

For in Jesus, my love for you is revealed. John 17:26

He is the exact representation of my being. Hebrews 1:3

He came to demonstrate that I am for you, not against you. Romans 8:31

And to tell you that I am not counting your sins. 2 Corinthians 5:18–19

Jesus died so that you and I could be reconciled. 2 Corinthians 5:18–19

His death was the ultimate expression of my love for you. 1 John 4:10

I gave up everything I loved that I might gain your love. Romans 8:31–32

If you receive the gift of my son, Jesus, you receive me. 1 John 2:23

And nothing will ever separate you from my love again. Romans 8:38–39

Come home and I'll throw the biggest party heaven has ever seen. Luke 15:7

I have always been Father, and will always be Father. Ephesians 3:14–15

My question is . . . Will you be my child? John 1:12–13

I am waiting for you. Luke 15:11–32

Love, Your Dad.
Almighty God

THE FATHER LOVES MY DAD

Throughout this book I have described my own father as a hard, drunken rogue. However, the heavenly Father determined a different ending for my dad. I wrote in my Bible study *Following God: Perplexing Proverbs for Women* the following result of the Father's love for my dad.

> *The antiseptic smell of the intensive care unit assaulted my nose as I sat next to my father's bed. Machines whirred and beeped with each labored breath he took. One collapsed lung along with the other full of pneumonia predicted the outcome for him.*
>
> *"So this is how it ends," I pondered. For years, a love-hate relationship with this man influenced many of my decisions. Some good, some bad. I always sought his approval, but rarely did he grant it.*
>
> *I struggled to believe my father could transform from a mean and bitter man to one full of love for others. But then one chilly October night he accepted Jesus Christ as his Savior. At the age of 79, my earthly father discovered the Father God's unconditional love. I couldn't believe it. I traveled five hundred miles just to look into those crinkled hazel eyes to see a new dad peering out at me. Our relationship changed drastically. Finally, my father became the dad I desired.*

The Father loves us. He embraces us. He is our Good Shepherd who seeks out the lost—even an elderly man with a lifetime of alcoholism and relational abuse. Our heavenly Father is asking us to dance for all eternity with His Son, Jesus Christ. Have you accepted His love? Will you dance with El-roi, the God who sees you? Will you allow Jehovah-tsidkenu to dress you in righteousness? Will you accept His invitation to the wedding of the Lamb — His Son — Jesus Christ — the Lord of all creation? Won't you trust in Christ today and receive eternal life?

THE END AND ONLY THE BEGINNING

At traditional wedding ceremonies, a father releases his beloved daughter into the hands of the waiting bridegroom. And one day our heavenly Father, with rejoicing, will put our hands into the Bridegroom's nail-scarred hand. We are the bride of Jesus Christ. Our Jesus is the everlasting, ever-loving Bridegroom.

> *Let us rejoice and be glad and give him glory! For the wedding of the Lamb has come, and his bride has made herself ready.... Then the angel said to me, "Write: 'Blessed are those who are invited to the wedding supper of the Lamb!'" And he added, "These are the true words of God"* (REVELATION 19:7, 9).

Our Father, our Abba, our Daddy loves and embraces us. He is the Father. His Son, Jesus Christ, is our Bridegroom. And Jesus dances us into endless love.

Go dance!

Dance Lesson

Read Luke 15:11–32.

Describe the three principal characters of this parable.

Who showed love, compassion, and forgiveness?

Describe the reaction of the father in verses 20–23.

How does this parable demonstrate the love of our heavenly Father?

Advanced Dance Lessons

Read John 15:8–17.

What command did Jesus give in verse 9?

What will be the result of this obedience? (v. 11).

Write out the commandment given in verse 12.

Do you think it is possible to "love each other" all the time? Why or why not?

How do you think our loving each other ties into the statement, "Then the Father will give you whatever you ask in my name" (v. 16)?

Embraced by the Father Journal Page

Reread "The Father's Love Letter" and then write a love letter to your heavenly Father — Abba.

~~~~~~

~~~~~~

~~~~~~

~~~~~~

~~~~~~

~~~~~~

~~~~~~

~~~~~~

~~~~~~

~~~~~~

~~~~~~

~~~~~~

~~~~~~

~~~~~~

~~~~~~

~~~~~~

~~~~~~

~~~~~~

~~~~~~

~~~~~~

Aramaic name: ABBA

Definition: DADDY

Modern translations:
DADDY, PAPA, DEAR FATHER

The Heavenly Father
invites you to share in His love
as the bride
in the wedding and marriage feast with His Son,
Jesus Christ.
The ceremony will be held in heaven at
an upcoming time.
Dance into endless love.
Please RSVP.

Then the angel said to me, "Write: 'Blessed are those who are invited to the wedding supper of the Lamb!'" And he added, "These are the true words of God" (REVELATION 19:9).

Finale

randpa, I don't know how to die. I just don't get it. How do you die?" she asked. "I am tired of battling all of this." Motioning for another dose of painkiller, Breana's waxen face relayed frustration. Her blond pageboy wig sat slightly askew as if to punctuate her question.

With an age-spotted, trembling hand, he patted her wig back into place. His eyes filled with tears as he shrugged his shoulders without an answer. No one in the room volunteered a response to the baffled 15-year-old, as her mom, Jayme, administered the needed pain relief.

After a 17-month grueling war with cancer, Breana faced her last battle. Death. Although her spirit remained indomitable, her young, previously athletic body could no longer continue fighting. Family, friends, pastors, and medical professionals circled around day after day in support.

Doctors had watched her win decisive victories over chemotherapy and radiation treatments. Respect filled their voices as they conferred with each other and spoke of her tenacity to bounce back. She amazed her family when she triumphed over each surgery and recovered her teenaged enthusiasm for life. Friends who came to give support found themselves cheered on by Breana in their own life struggles.

Pastors turned her story into sermons illustrating a walk of faith and trust, although not one of them knew the answer to her question, "How do I die?"

However, the Lord God knew the answer to her dilemma. Before the question popped from her lips, the answer was on its way.

The doorbell rang. A neighbor stood at the doorway and appeared unsure of herself. She said, "I hope this doesn't seem too presumptuous, but I feel the Lord wanted me to bring this book to Breana." She offered in an extended hand a sky blue book. The title, *Heaven: Your Real Home*, jumped out as Breana's mom reached for it.

"Thank you," Jayme replied politely — uncertain of what she thought of the gift.

She walked to back to Breana's side and placed the book into her thin hand. Immediately, Breana began to scan the table of contents. Then intrigued, she read a few pages. The author, Joni Eareckson Tada, described the reality and delight of heaven with clarity. She wrote eagerly and expectantly of her own desire of heaven.

With a slurred, medicated voice Breana said, "Well, even if I don't know how to die, I guess heaven will be more than I can imagine. This book brings me peace, Mom."

However, the book was only a part of God's answer to her question of how to die. Within the community, groups met weekly to pray for Breana and her family. One night in prayer, God nudged Laura, a local artist, to draw a picture for Breana.

Inspired, she began the charcoal drawing immediately. She drew; she erased. She pondered and prayed. She drew and erased again. As the charcoal pencil flew across the paper, it seemed as God directed each detail. Laura penciled at a frenzied pace. She felt compelled to complete the picture. Within days, the work of art sat finished, framed, and ready for delivery.

Meanwhile, each time Breana felt anxiety, she requested the book, which she had renamed her "Peace Book." She read it to herself. She read portions to anyone who sat by her bed. Calmness crept into her wan face. Still she wondered, *How do I die? How do I step from this world into heaven?*

The doorbell rang. Once again, a hesitant friend stood holding a gift. Handing over a large wrapped package, she greeted Breana's mother nervously. "Hi, Jayme. This is from someone who wants to remain anonymous. We hope it blesses Breana and your family." Fumbling for words, she finished with, "We feel this gift was directed by God."

Once again, Jayme walked across to her daughter's bedside. Breana's dark-circled eyes watched expectantly as her mom undid the wrapping around the package. The entire family gasped as they stared at the picture. It was a portrait of Breana dressed in a bridal gown gliding down a path to meet a groom.

In the picture, Breana stood tall and straight in a floor-length, white bridal dress. Elegant, yet simple, it revealed flawless skin. The skin showed no weaving of surgical scars. A flowing lacy veil hung gracefully from her head to her bare feet. It seemed as if a halo of pure health enveloped her.

However, it was Breana's face that mesmerized everyone. Her countenance reflected the anticipation of bridal joy. Her eyes sparkled. Breana's smile radiated with such completeness that everything else paled in comparison. She was smiling at the groom.

The groom's head was turned toward Breana. Upon His head sat a stately crown. A robe draped His broad shoulders with a sash that read, "King of kings and Lord and lords."

As Breana's awed family studied the picture, they noticed a small rock wall that ran behind the path. Upon the ledge lay a small blue book. The side binding revealed the title, *Peace Book*. Breana appeared to pass by it without a second glance. Her shining eyes looked toward an outstretched nail-scarred hand. The bride saw only the Groom beckoning for her.

Then the doorbell chimed again.

This time high school friends trooped in and circled Breana's chair. It was prom night. Dressed in sparkly dresses, they crowded around for Jayme to take their pictures together with Breana. Enjoying her friends' excitement and youthful enthusiasm, Breana pointed to her portrait with a weak grin.

"My dress," she struggled to say.

"It's beautiful! Oh, you look gorgeous!"

She nodded wistfully.

As her friends left, Breana pondered the picture. An elusive message seemed to emit from it.

"Oh well, I just don't get it. I'm tired. Mom, I want to go to sleep."

A fitful night ensued. Breana mumbled unintelligible words. Sitting on the edge of the bed, Jayme asked, "Do you want your Peace Book?" Shaking her head, Breana appeared confused and disoriented.

A final time a doorbell tinkled faintly from a distance.

Suddenly, in a clear, healthy voice, Breana said, "I get it! I get it!"

"What is it? What do you get?" Jayme asked anxiously.

Breana stared wide-eyed into the darkness of the bedroom and said, "He's watching me."

"Is it Jesus, Breana?"

Speechless, she nodded.

Crying, Breana's mom said, "Take His hand, baby. Take His hand."

Jayme lifted the bride's battle-worn hand into the air and placed it into the Groom's invisible hand. A sigh of satisfaction escaped from the bride's lips as she started down the path with her Groom to eternal life.

Although Jayme could not see her, Breana, more radiant than in life, turned, lifted her hand, and waved good-bye. She parted her fingers in a V to signal peace and victory. She had her answer. She knew how to die. Breana had won the final battle. The bride began to dance with the Groom. One, two, three, one, two . . .

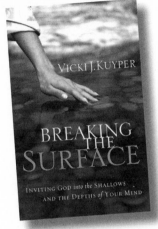
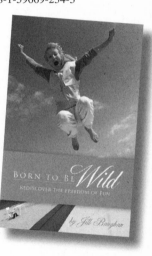

New Hope® Publishers is a division of WMU®,
an international organization that challenges Christian believers to
understand and be radically involved in God's mission.
For more information about WMU, go to www.wmu.com.

More information about New Hope books may be found
at www.newhopepublishers.com.
New Hope books may be purchased at your local bookstore.

*If you've been blessed by this book, we would like to hear
your story. The publisher and author welcome your
comments and suggestions at: newhopereader@wmu.org.*